We wish you a
FELIZ NAVIDAD
2017
and a *MUCHO* better
NEW YEAR!

HARVEY HOUSES
of NEW MEXICO

Historic Hospitality from Raton to Deming

ROSA WALSTON LATIMER

THE
History
PRESS

Published by The History Press
Charleston, SC 29403
www.historypress.net

First published 2015

Manufactured in the United States

ISBN 978.1.62619.859.3

Library of Congress Control Number: 2015932933

Lovingly dedicated to
Gertrude McCormick Balmanno,
my Harvey Girl grandmother who gave me New Mexico roots,
and
William Crosby (Uncle Bill) Balmanno.
Thank you for giving me a family history!

CONTENTS

FOREWORD

At last—a book that is only about the Harvey Girls, especially the Harvey Girls of New Mexico. When I met Rosa Latimer, author of *Harvey Houses of Texas: Historic Hospitality from the Gulf Coast to the Panhandle*, she told me she had found in her research that there were many Harvey Girls whose names and stories could not be found in any one place. When she came to our Belen Harvey House Museum to continue her research, we spent ten hours researching while she and her daughter, Lara, copied and scanned hundreds of pieces from our archives. As each piece came out of the archive boxes, I couldn't help but remember when it came into our collection.

I was introduced to Fred Harvey, the Harvey Girls, the Santa Fe Railroad and local history when I moved to Belen, New Mexico, twenty plus years ago and became a museum volunteer in an original 1910 Harvey House. Our Harvey House was a lunchroom and dining room for forty years and then became a Santa Fe Reading Room for railroaders for another forty years afterward. The history was there in the building; we just had to discover it. When the Santa Fe gave the building to the city, a room was set aside for a historical museum. By listening to visitors and reading the archives already in the building, we volunteers became acquainted with its history. On a regular basis, we added to the collection as visitors shared with us their life experiences and connections to our history.

It was a treasured memory when two former Harvey Girls—Opal Fuqua and Irene Armstrong, who lived in Belen—visited with their families. They came from the Midwest and had married railroad men. Their pictures are on exhibit, and their audio stories are in the archives.

There have been dozens of volunteers working as docents who became enthusiastic about telling the stories found in our exhibits. It was very special when former Harvey Girls from near and far—or their families—visited and were encouraged to tell the stories of their experiences. The most common comment from the Harvey Girls was that each one thought her decision to leave home and sign up to come west as a Harvey Girl was the best thing she could have done.

In 2006, the museum started the Red Log Book. We had visitors write their Fred Harvey/Santa Fe employee stories in the book for the museum archives. The visitors would look back through the book to read what had been written and it would remind them of the experiences that they wanted to share. These comments are a treasure for the museum.

Through the years, the museum has been represented at the annual conferences of the New Mexico Association of Museums and the New Mexico Historical Society. Networking at these conferences has brought recognition and interest to our Harvey House Museum and the Fred Harvey/Harvey Girls story.

I have visited Harvey Houses along the Santa Fe railroad from New Mexico through Kansas, from New Mexico to California and from New Mexico to Rosenburg, Texas. It is fascinating to think of all the young women who were Harvey Girls in these places—because you were a Harvey Girl for the rest of your life even if you only worked for three months one summer before you married or went on to further your education.

Recently, there was an obituary for the Red Log Book. Billie Roger was ninety-five years old. She was a Harvey Girl from the early 1950s to the late 1970s. An era is passing but not forgotten.

MAURINE MCMILLAN, EMERITUS DIRECTOR
Harvey House Museum
Belen, New Mexico

ACKNOWLEDGEMENTS

Rediscovering my New Mexico roots while writing this book has been a delightful experience, providing me a stronger connection to my family and its history. The interesting, delightful folks I met who have a genuine interest in preserving and sharing history made the venture more enjoyable.

Thank you to the following individuals for their help in obtaining information and images: Patt Leonard, Jack Kelly, Everet Apodaca, John Valdes, Louise Reynolds and family, Carrie Cygan, Sandy Whittley, Don Williams and Sylvia Ligocky of the Luna County Historical Society and Meredith Davidson of the New Mexico History Museum.

Without the help and support of Michael McMillan and his fabulous vintage postcard collection, I could not have properly told this story. How fortunate I am to be acquainted with this very talented, knowledgeable individual. Thank you for sharing, Michael!

The entire staff of Belen Harvey House Museum and Maurine McMillan were especially helpful in sharing the treasure-trove of Fred Harvey information held in the archives of the museum. Thank you also to Dr. Eric Blinman of the New Mexico Office of Archaeological Studies.

I'm grateful to Danyelle Gentry Petersen and Beau Gentry for sharing the story of their father, Skip Gentry. By all accounts, Skip was a great friend to all who knew him, and his collection of Fred Harvey/Harvey House memorabilia is unsurpassed. We are fortunate to have some of Beau's photos of some pieces from Skip's collection included in this book.

A special shout out to Jim and Kathy Weir! I count their friendship as one of the valuable, unexpected benefits of writing this book. I'm looking forward to more Fred Harvey/Mary Colter adventures with these two special people.

Thank you to Kathy Hendrickson of the Las Vegas Citizens Committee for Historical Preservation and Cindy Collins of Main Street de Las Vegas for your support.

Many, many thanks to Janice Plummer for looking after all my critters and generally making my life better, to Kathy Beach for being a wonderful traveling companion and to Melissa Morrow for her encouragement and wisdom during this project. Also, my warm regards to Dana Smith, whose early support of my writing projects continues to be the foundation of my work.

To my daughter and best friend, Lara: I love you and am so thankful to have you in my life. Thank you for all you do to make everything better for me.

In all things I have done since meeting "His Happiness," I acknowledge his unfailing love, which continues to be a profound presence in my life.

INTRODUCTION

M y interest in Harvey Girls began when I learned that my grandmother had been a Harvey Girl in Rincon, New Mexico. My uncle, who shared this information with me, was obviously very proud of his mother's achievement, and I didn't have a clue what a Harvey Girl was! As I began to learn more, I realized the importance of these women in the history of our country. I also realized that there were many like me who did not know the remarkable story of Fred Harvey and the Harvey Girls.

The writing of this book—as well as my previous book, *Harvey Houses of Texas*—is my way of paying tribute to my grandmother, a woman somewhat mysterious to me, as I last saw her when I was two years old. This is also my way of recognizing the young women who answered Fred Harvey's advertisements for "educated women of good character" to work in Harvey Houses, many of whom lived when acceptable careers for a young woman were limited to teacher or nurse. It was a time when working as a waitress was not considered a respectable occupation for young, single women.

It is generally thought that over 100,000 women worked as Harvey Girls from the late nineteenth century to the 1940s, when most of the Harvey restaurants had closed. A few Harvey Houses in New Mexico remained open until the late 1940s, and the Alvarado in Albuquerque continued serving train passengers until 1969. The Fred Harvey company sold the La Fonda in Santa Fe in 1968, and even though there are no longer Harvey Girls, La Fonda continues to provide excellent food and service.

Left to right: Harvey Girls Frieda Baumgartner, Mary Counties and Hazel Clayton with an unidentified Harvey House pantry boy standing trackside in Gallup, New Mexico, circa 1933. *Courtesy of Baumgartner-Leonard Collection.*

When Fred Harvey handpicked waitresses, dressed them in starched uniforms and sent them out to feed the traveling public, I am not sure he realized how Harvey Girls would change the course of history. Many were the first to venture more than walking distance from their hometown. Others had traveled extensively and recognized the prospect of adventure in the West. Surely, the Harvey Girl hopefuls were all keenly aware that working in a remote place where few women lived would provide many opportunities for meeting prospective husbands.

New Mexico Harvey Girl Emily Hahn may have best explained why so many answered Fred Harvey's call with the title of her book: *Nobody Said Not to Go*. Emily, who says she traveled across the United States in the 1920s dressed as a boy before becoming a Harvey Girl, had many adventures during her lifetime, all because "nobody said not to go."

I can imagine there were many times when a young woman's mother, under the stern gaze of a protective father, would not say "Go!," but who also did not say "Don't go." Perhaps the older woman had yearned for adventure at a young age and realized this chance to be a Harvey Girl was hope for a better life for her daughter. Even if parents encouraged their daughter to seize the opportunity, their attitude may have changed when, after six months or a year, they received a letter announcing marriage to a Santa Fe brakeman or a rancher.

Harvey Girls worked hard, had fun and made Fred Harvey proud. Through the years, their income usually exceeded what was paid in other professions. The women sent money home to help their families through the Depression years or paid for a college education, leading some to careers in archaeology and journalism.

For every personal story in this book, there are hundreds more that would help us remember the difficult decisions, the adventurous spirit and the desire to perform a job with pride that brought young women to New Mexico and brought New Mexican women to Harvey Houses.

Certainly, Fred Harvey had a unique vision for restaurants along the railroad and was an astute businessman, as were his sons and grandsons who continued the business after Mr. Harvey's death. However, it was the employees, led by Harvey Girls, who made the Fred Harvey company a success. It is my hope that this book will help carve a broader niche in New Mexico history for these spirited, hardworking women.

NEW MEXICO HARVEY HOUSES

✴Raton

✴Gallup

✴Santa Fe ✴Las Vegas
✴Lamy

✴Albuquerque

✴Belen ✴Vaughn

✴
Clovis

✴San Marcial

✴Rincon

✴Deming ✴Las Cruces

New Mexico Harvey House locations. *Map by Melissa Morrow.*

Chapter 1
FRED HARVEY IN NEW MEXICO

The land of desert and stars, modern and ancient cultures, forest green and rocky tan.
—Hospitality Magazine: A Magazine For and About the
Men and Women of Fred Harvey

Fred Harvey's narrative in the United States began when the Englishman immigrated in 1850 at the age of fifteen. Harvey learned the restaurant business working as a pot scrubber and busboy in New York. Later, he owned a café in St. Louis, Missouri, that catered to wealthy businessmen who expected fast service and good food served in tasteful surroundings. However, the effects of the Civil War and a dishonest partner brought an end to his first restaurant venture. Harvey then found employment with the railroad as a freight agent, solicitor and mail clerk and traveled many miles by rail. This experience provided firsthand knowledge of how difficult it was to get decent food while traveling by train. This insider information would serve him very well.

Mr. Harvey knew the Santa Fe Railroad was expanding and needed to develop a robust passenger business to finance the growth. With his knowledge of the restaurant business, he believed he could help accomplish this. When Harvey met with Santa Fe officials in 1876, the entrepreneur was confident he could personally change the miserable reputation of railway dining and increase passenger service. On a handshake with the president of the Santa Fe Railroad, an agreement was reached, and the first restaurant chain in the United States was launched.

Fred Harvey, founder of Harvey House restaurants, newsstands and hotels. Harvey is credited for bringing a high standard of hospitality to towns along the Santa Fe Railroad. *Courtesy of kansasmemory.org, Kansas State Historical Society.*

As Fred Harvey's chain of trackside restaurants grew, when a location was deemed appropriate for a Harvey establishment, the Santa Fe would design and build space in or adjacent to the new depot building for the kitchen, food storage, a lunch counter and usually a dining room, as well as living quarters for Harvey employees. This space, built especially for Fred Harvey's business venture, was called a Harvey House. Mr. Harvey was also afforded the use of Santa Fe trains to deliver laundry, food products and employees along the line at no charge.

Originally Harvey Houses were established along the railroad at intervals of approximately one hundred miles, providing dining opportunities for passengers when the train stopped to refuel the steam engine. Other sites were determined by the location of Santa Fe division points where large numbers of railroad employees needed a place to eat.

In New Mexico, the Fred Harvey story is more than a tale of first-class eating establishments along the Santa Fe Railroad. When Fred Harvey made his sales pitch to the president of the Santa Fe, he proposed restaurants with such stellar food and service that people would ride the train just so they could eat at a Harvey House. That vision motivated the building of luxury hotels with amenities that catered to tourists giving them a destination with Harvey House restaurants, luxury accommodations, lush patios for rest and relaxation and a cultural experience.

The development of tourism by the Fred Harvey company was an intelligent business decision that had a lasting impact on New Mexico. The emphasis on tourism in the state continues. In 2014, the New Mexico governor's office reported a third consecutive year of tourism growth, with 32.2 million people traveling to the state in 2013.

The Fred Harvey company valued consistent food quality as much as quality of service. Only the best, freshly prepared food was offered at a Harvey House, and travelers soon realized they could trust the Fred Harvey name all along the Santa Fe line.

Harvey House managers were required to send tabulated reports at the end of each day. The purpose of these reports was not to assess possible ways of reducing expenses but to ensure that the Harvey standard was maintained. *Santa Fe* magazine explained that the reports made certain "the slices of ham in the Harvey sandwiches are as thick as ever and the same thickness everywhere and that the coffee is as strong as it should be." In Harvey Houses, whole pies were cut into four servings instead of the usual six or eight in other restaurants. The daily reports reflected the inventory of food used in relation to the number of customers served, indicating that portions were up to Harvey standards. Many Harvey Houses operated in the red for years. Fred Harvey's business philosophy was simple. He believed that profits would come in the long run if excellent service was provided and maintained.

Fred Harvey died in 1901 at the age of sixty-five. That year, he owned and operated approximately fifteen hotels, forty-seven restaurants, thirty dining cars and a San Francisco Bay ferry. The eulogy delivered at his funeral foretold the way Fred Harvey would always be remembered. "Fred Harvey is dead, but his spirit still lives. The standard of excellence he set can never go back. He has been a civilizer and benefactor. He has added to the physical, mental and spiritual welfare of millions. Fred Harvey simply kept faith with the public. He gave pretty nearly a perfect service."

After his death, Harvey's sons, Ford and Byron, continued to operate the substantial family business, and the company name remained "Fred Harvey." For years, employees continued to say they worked for Fred Harvey.

Business at Harvey Houses began to decline during the Depression years and continued to falter even as the nation recovered economically. The increase of dining cars (usually staffed and operated by the same Fred Harvey company) made it unnecessary for passengers to leave the train to eat, and diesel engines were replacing steam locomotives, eliminating the need for frequent fuel stops. In addition, the automobile was becoming a popular and affordable way to travel. Many Harvey Houses closed; however, when troops were mobilized during World War II, thousands traveled by passenger train, and Fred Harvey's restaurants were reopened to provide meals to these U.S. armed forces. Former Harvey Girls and other employees returned to work in the Harvey Houses that had been closed, and in locations still open, such as the Alvarado in Albuquerque, additional staff was hired to handle the increased business.

In reality, the thousands of troops traveling by train added greatly to the Harvey House customer base during the time when civilian train travel was waning, bringing profits back to some sites that had been closed for several years. The results of a smart, extensive marketing effort, coupled with the enduring Harvey reputation and an increase in patrons, were positive for the company. According to intercompany memos, Fred Harvey served over forty-one million meals and brought in a gross income of over $37 million in 1945, the largest in the company's seventy-year history.

Harvey Girls

There is a difference between eating and dining. Fred Harvey brought dining to New Mexico accompanied by an appreciation for the land and culture of the West. He also brought Harvey Girls.

Originally, Harvey attempted to staff Harvey Houses with local, all-male employees. This led to many problems, not the least of which was an unwillingness or inability to meet the high Fred Harvey standards. A pivotal event in Raton, New Mexico, brought a change that proved to be extremely successful. Following an incident at the Raton Harvey House that left the all-male staff unable to work the next morning, an enraged Fred Harvey fired everyone and hired a new manager who suggested replacing the unruly men with attractive young women. Harvey agreed, and ads began to appear in the northeast and midwest similar to this:

> *Wanted—Young women, 18–30 years of age, of good character, attractive, and intelligent, as waitresses in Harvey Eating Houses on the Santa Fe Railroad in the West. Good wages, with room and meals furnished. Experience not necessary. Write Fred Harvey, Union Depot, Kansas City, Missouri.*

In the early years, all young women who answered the ad traveled to Kansas City for a rigorous personal interview. For a number of years, Alice Steel conducted many of these interviews. Alice is remembered fondly by some Harvey Girls as being sympathetic and understanding; however, others found her to be stern and somewhat harsh. In either case,

New Mexico Harvey Girl Bertha Peterson (second from right) with unidentified Harvey Girls. *Courtesy of Carrie Cygan.*

this initial interview looms large in the memory of many Harvey Girls. Alice's impression of a young lady determined whether the black-and-white uniform was in her future. Later, interviews were also conducted in Chicago, and as the West became more populated and trusted Harvey managers were in place, more local women were hired.

Regardless of the hiring process, once on the job, Harvey Girls were held to strict standards. Harvey's precise rules about dressing modestly, wearing little or no makeup and conducting oneself in a respectable manner served the purpose of reassuring young ladies that they would be in good company, working and living with like-minded women. Their reputations would be protected even far from home where they would often be judged without benefit of a family's good reputation.

Harvey Girls personalized the Fred Harvey standards and, in many cases, brought their eastern and midwestern sensibilities to a job that previously was not held in high esteem. Harvey's rules were a dominant part of any Harvey Girl's experience and served to standardize service in Harvey Houses. The expectation that Harvey Girls conduct themselves in a ladylike manner at all times changed the public perception of waitresses.

The ambitious, venturesome young women who had successful interviews were given a train pass to their new jobs and often left immediately. Most began their Harvey Girl career at a smaller Harvey House such as Rincon or Vaughn, New Mexico. In the early years, all Harvey Girls were single and were required to sign a contract stipulating they would not marry during the first six months of employment. Eventually, married women were hired, and in unusual circumstances, a widow with a child was permitted to live and work at a New Mexico Harvey House.

Much has been written about the many couples who met across the counter in a Harvey House and eventually married. However, most

Publicity photograph for the 1946 movie *The Harvey Girls*, featuring Judy Garland. *Author's collection.*

Harvey Girls were very particular about who they allowed to "court" them and even more picky when it came time to choose a husband. A former Harvey Girl recalled her engagement to a Santa Fe engineer. The couple had the Harvey House manager's approval, and the relationship seemed headed to the altar until the prospective groom grew a mustache. The young woman didn't like kissing a man with facial hair, and she told her fiancé she wouldn't marry him unless he shaved. He didn't, and she didn't marry him.

Many people became familiar with Harvey Girls through the 1946 MGM movie *The Harvey Girls.* The movie, set in a fictitious New Mexico town, featured top movie stars of the time—Judy Garland, Ray Bolger and Angela Lansbury—and can still be seen occasionally on the Turner Classic Movies channel. The song "On the Atchison, Topeka and the Santa Fe," sung by Garland, won an Academy Award for songwriter Johnnie Mercer. The movie was filmed on a movie set in California, and the set design was modeled from the exterior and dining room of the Castaneda, a Harvey hotel in Las Vegas, New Mexico. According to movie trivia, the balcony featured in one of the movie's musical numbers is a replica of Castaneda's street-side, second-floor balcony. Apparently, during the time Harvey Girls were working at Castaneda, there was a saloon directly across the street. In the movie, the Alhambra saloon was across the dirt street from the fictitious New Mexico Harvey House.

Southwest Indian Detours

As train passenger service improved, traveling to New Mexico became much more comfortable and accessible. Those who lived in other parts of the United States began to travel west for vacations. Many credit the Fred Harvey company with developing commercial cultural tourism. Fred Harvey Indian Detours complemented the established Harvey hotels and restaurants and became the bedrock for tourism in the Southwest.

The imaginative Indian Detours gave train passengers a reason to interrupt their train trip and take excursions by car (known as Harveycars) or Indian Detour buses to local attractions, including Indian pueblos and Spanish mission ruins. Young women, called Couriers, were trained in the history of the area and served as tour guides. Perhaps not as well remembered as Harvey Girls, the Couriers were an important part of the success of the Indian Detours. A review

A New Mexico Indian Detour driver. The Harvey tours provided sightseeing trips to living pueblos and archaeological sites throughout the Southwest. *Courtesy Belen Harvey House Museum Photo Archives.*

of the Indian Detours in the *New York Times* magazine described one Courier: "Our guide tells the tale, a pretty young college girl in high boots and a 10-gallon hat, with enough Indian jewelry to open a curio shop." These uniforms added to the charm of the Detours, but the attractive young women were expected to be in every way as prepared for their job as the Harvey Girls were. The Harveycar motor cruises allowed visitors, traveling in enormous cars with sixteen cylinders, to experience the many cultures of the Southwest. Fred Harvey advertising invited tourists to take "roads to yesterday" and travel "back through the centuries."

Marketing for the Indian Detours touted the unknown paths of the Indians "worn inches deep in solid rock by moccasined feet; the ways of the sandaled padres and steel-clad soldiers of Spain; the trails of the fur-capped mountain men; and the broad tracks blazed by those in buckskin and deepened under the dust clouds of plodding pack trains and covered wagons." Who wouldn't want to leave the constraints of train travel to experience this? Many took advantage of this "southwestern motor service designed for the most discriminating traveler."

According to company records, the Detours served 150,000 square miles in southwestern Colorado, New Mexico and Arizona. The good reputation of Fred Harvey was the primary marketing strategy: "The interest of the railroad, and the management of the Harvey company, assure efficiency in personnel, the finest of equipment and that type of finely individual services so long a source of pride with the parent organizations."

Detour itineraries were often mixed with horseback riding and camping. The Detours are evidence of the continued business acumen of the Fred Harvey company. (Enjoy a sample of a 1920 Indian Detour via a fifteen-minute film posted on YouTube by the Office of Image Archaeology.)

Indian Department and Museum

Herman Schweizer was a German immigrant who worked as a railroad newsboy and was soon considered one of the Harvey system's brightest young men. Obviously Fred Harvey trusted him, as Herman was sent, at the age of sixteen, to a Harvey House in Coolidge, New Mexico, when Harvey found the establishment was not meeting company standards. While at the remote Harvey House location, the young man often rode through the Navajo and Hopi reservations. Soon he had established a relationship with the local craftsmen and traders and began to sell their products at the Harvey House.

Schweizer was encouraged by Minnie Harvey Huckel, Fred Harvey's daughter, to develop a museum of southwestern arts and crafts at the Alvarado in Albuquerque, New Mexico. He rose to the position of manager of the Fred Harvey Indian Department, a position he held until his death in 1943.

The Indian Department revived and preserved ancient tribal arts of the Hopi, Navajo and Zuni. Eventually, this undertaking became the Fred Harvey Fine Arts Collection, thousands of pieces of Indian and Spanish Colonial artifacts, most

A typical wool Navajo rug sold in the Fred Harvey Indian Building at the Alvarado in Albuquerque, New Mexico. *Photo by Beau Gentry. Courtesy of Skip Gentry's Fred Harvey Memorabilia Collection.*

A Fred Harvey tag on an item guaranteeing it as an authentic Native American product. *Photo by Beau Gentry. Courtesy of Skip Gentry's Fred Harvey Memorabilia Collection.*

of which were given to the Heard Museum in Phoenix, Arizona.

The Harvey Indian Department's emphasis on handmade Indian blankets, rugs, jewelry and pottery brought prosperity to Indian artisans and was so successful that the Santa Fe Railroad incorporated Indian motifs into its advertising and merchandising.

Trains arriving in Albuquerque stopped in front of the depot, and passengers could not reach the main Alvarado hotel without first passing the Indian Building. In this space, designed by Fred Harvey designer Mary Colter, visitors discovered a museum, sales rooms and artists demonstrating their work. The La Fonda Harvey hotel in Santa Fe, New Mexico, had an Indian Room, and smaller Indian curio shops were adapted in other Harvey House locations.

A taped interview with Navajo Oakee James from the American Indian Oral History Collection in the Center for Southwest Research at the University of New Mexico explains how the Harvey/Navajo partnership developed:

Well, the story begins that until the railroad came the Navajo had been living in an old fashioned world. Traveling in groups in new machine had long ago sweep the whites into another kind of class. In 1883 when the railroad came, the same kind of change began for the Navajo; the change came so slowly that at first the people could not see what was happening.

Most Navajo had no money and in fact, had never used what they had—sheepskins and wools and blankets. If they brought these to the store, trader could give them groceries, clothes and guns. The Navajo wove in blankets and he would sell to eastern store and factory. Wool did not always bring a good price for the Navajo were still hooking it off with a knife, and sometimes when the sheep were half starving, the wool was very thin. Also, the heavy waterproof blankets with their strap were not suitable to use on eastern beds. Then one of the whites had an idea, no one even remembers now whether they…this was a trader or a missionary or government worker, but they remember the idea which made such a great difference to the Navajo. Why not make the blankets heavier and thinner so that they could be used as floor rugs? That idea set the Navajo woman up in a business that was to bring in millions of dollars. The weavers was for trade and like good business woman made what the buyers wanted [sic].

These buyers were all tourists who passed through the Southwest by the hundreds. The Santa Fe Railroad was in full running order, all the way to the Pacific Coast. Eating houses were set up along the line, running by the famous Fred Harvey Hotel Line, Santa Fe Railroad today. The travelers were not only army officers and businessmen taking dangerous trips because they had to…they sometimes came to see the country or to look for a place to settle. They were interested in Indian goods and wanted to take some home.

Prior to the creation of the Indian Department, native artisans took advantage of train stops on their reservations as an opportunity to sell their goods to passing travelers. With the creation of the Indian Department, Native Americans became employed as salespeople and demonstrators at Harvey hotels across the Southwest. The sale of pottery, jewelry and textiles in partnership with the Fred Harvey company along with employment with the railroad had a long-lasting, positive impact on the economy of Native American communities.

In 1952, the Fred Harvey company employee publication *Hospitality* paid tribute to the Harvey operations in New Mexico and Arizona as part of the company's seventy-fifth anniversary celebration: "For it was here in the land of desert and stars, modern and ancient cultures, forest green and rocky tan that the Fred Harvey organization grew up. Here was the area in which Fred Harvey's reputation flourished early, and where it is still dominant."

Only a third of the New Mexico Harvey Houses have survived, but the influence of the many dedicated Harvey employees who instilled the Fred Harvey "way" into the fiber of the state remains today.

Chapter 2

STAY AWHILE

Destination Harvey Hotels

As the railroad developed in New Mexico, the rugged terrain and diverse culture provided the perfect setting to expand the Harvey House experience and establish luxury hotels with tourist attractions. These hotels became favorite stops for train passengers headed to the West Coast and served as a home base for vacationers who enjoyed the

Guests at the Alvarado in Albuquerque, New Mexico, enjoyed lounging on the lush trackside patio. *Courtesy of Michael McMillan.*

first-rate accommodations while exploring the surrounding environment. The luxurious destination Harvey hotels had it all: interesting architecture, colorful design, the allure of native artists, delicious freshly prepared food and outstanding service, all presented in the well-known Fred Harvey way.

Alvarado

Albuquerque

Wherever there is a Harvey House, civilization is not far behind.
—1946 MGM movie The Harvey Girls

Perhaps the most celebrated opening of a Harvey House in New Mexico was the Alvarado in Albuquerque. Built for $200,000 in 1902, a year after Fred Harvey's death, the hotel and surrounding buildings were known as the "Gray Lady" along the tracks at First Street. And what a lady she was! The California Mission style of architecture featured towers, balconies and arcades supported by dramatic, turquoise-trimmed arches. Replacing a simple Harvey House that had opened in 1883, the hotel complex included the popular Indian Building, along with the Santa Fe depot, and stretched seven hundred feet north and south along the railroad tracks. The name "Alvarado" was taken from the name of a Spanish artillery captain on the Coronado expedition through the Southwest, Don Hernando de Alvarado.

The Alvarado was the first project with the Fred Harvey company for architect Mary Colter. Using a mix of Spanish and American Indian influence, she established a distinctive style that was used in other Harvey hotels and

The Alvarado in Albuquerque, New Mexico. The Fred Harvey hotel opened in 1902 with seventy-five guest rooms. *Courtesy of Michael McMillan.*

restaurants in the Southwest. Colter's legendary imprint on the Indian Building in particular provided the perfect setting for the museum and sales rooms.

Navajo Oakee James described the Indian Building in an interview recorded for the American Indian Oral History Collection:

> *It was Fred Harvey who decided to teach these travelers how to know a really good Navajo rug and to exchange with the Navajo to make them. He and the Santa Fe Railroad established the Indian House at Albuquerque. Here, tourists getting out of the train for a few minutes could see Navajo woman weaving and he taught how fine and difficult the art was…Rugs were hung around the room with signs to show which had the good yarn and the wool rug and which were poor and which were made by machine. Rug weaving was a paying business from the beginning.*

A visitor in 1916 wrote this description of a visit to the Alvarado in his travel journal:

> *After breakfasting we approached the curio rooms—Indian, Spanish and Mexican historic and prehistoric relics. From the railroad, the approach to these rooms is lined with Indians selling pottery. Should you attempt to kodak them they cover their heads with shawls, but if you tip them you may take their picture.*

The Harvey business in Albuquerque wasn't all about exotic art and tourists. A large laundry with almost sixty employees was located there. Large laundry facilities also were in Newton, Kansas; Needles, California; Temple, Texas; and at the Grand Canyon. These important, practical links in the Fred Harvey organization handled laundry for the entire Harvey system of restaurants and hotels. The system laundered over one million pieces each month and, at times, had to utilize other commercial laundries to handle overflow of uniforms and linens. One benefit Harvey Girls enjoyed was being able to send their uniforms out to be laundered. Uniforms were expected to be sparkling clean at all times, which often meant changing several times during a busy shift. Explaining this luxury to me, one Harvey Girl said, "We'd put the dirty uniforms in a large canvas basket. They sent it on the train to the nearest laundry and my uniforms would come back clean and starched in a couple of days. All I had to do was iron them. I was living in the lap of luxury!"

To further enhance an authentic Southwest experience, the strict black-and-white Harvey Girl uniforms were often replaced with colorful, more festive uniforms. Waitresses in the Alvarado hotel dining room wore long,

A canvas laundry basket used to ship Harvey Girl uniforms and table linens by train from Albuquerque, New Mexico, to the Harvey laundry facility in Newton, Kansas. *Photo by Beau Gentry. Courtesy of Skip Gentry's Fred Harvey Memorabilia Collection.*

full, tiered skirts with peasant-style blouses. Harvey Girls in the lunchroom and coffee shop dressed in traditional uniforms.

The Alvarado closed in 1969, and the building was demolished in 1970 after local residents were unable to raise the $1.5 million the railroad was asking for the empty building. The story of the destruction of the Alvarado reminds me of the chorus of the Joni Mitchell song "Big Yellow Taxi," which was written and first recorded the same year the Alvarado was torn down:

> *Don't it always seem to go*
> *That you don't know what you've got*
> *Till it's gone*
> *They paved paradise*
> *And put up a parking lot*

Although Mitchell was referring to the destruction of the Garden of Allah, a popular Hollywood hotel known for its parties, the singer/

Street scene on First Street in front of the Alvarado in Albuquerque, New Mexico. *Courtesy of Michael McMillan.*

songwriter has explained that the lyrics are about taking things for granted and then missing them when they're gone. The Alvarado hotel in Albuquerque has certainly been missed.

Mention the Harvey Houses of New Mexico to a group of history-savvy folks, and someone is sure to lament the loss of the Alvarado. However, many believe the demolition of this Harvey Hotel sparked pride in historic sites and buildings in the state and influenced the preservation of many other historically significant structures.

The Alvarado might not have been paradise, but it was a very appealing luxury hotel and eating establishment that served train passengers and Albuquerque residents for over sixty years. One of six New Mexico luxury hotels built by the Fred Harvey company, the Alvarado was a popular destination or "stop-over" for many celebrities for several decades until the rich and famous began to travel by airplane. Photo archives of the Albuquerque Museum contain many images of celebrities such as Hedda Hopper, Rudolph Valentino and the Little Rascals trackside at the Alvarado. Most of the photos were taken by William Steele Dean, who could be characterized as an early paparazzo. Dean was the organist who accompanied silent films at Albuquerque's KiMo Theatre and was quite familiar with the film stars of the day. He often walked the short distance to

FRED HARVEY STANDARD RECIPE				
ITEM Gold Lion Dressing		PRODUCTION		DATE 4/16/58
PORTIONS	COST PER ( )		PORTION SIZE	CARD 154

PREPARATION AND SERVICE

Ingredients in Order of Mixing	1 Quart	1 Gallon	
Eggs, Beaten	2	8	1. Combine Beaten Eggs, lemon juice and worchestershire sauce
Lemon Juice	1½ oz.	6 oz.	
Garlic Cloves, Grated	3	12	2. Add salad oil slowly, continually beating mixture.
Worchestershire Sauce	1 tsp	4 tsp.	
Salad Oil	1½ pints	3 qts.	
Grated Parmesan Cheese	3 oz.	12 oz.	3. Add cheese and remaining spices, salt and pepper to taste.
A-1 Sauce	1 tsp.	4 tsp.	
Tabasco Sauce	To Taste	To Taste	
Maggi Liquid	To Taste	To Taste	

Gold Lion Dressing   No. 154

Recipe for Gold Lion Dressing on an original Fred Harvey Standard Recipe card. *Courtesy of Belen Harvey House Museum.*

the Santa Fe Depot and Alvarado hotel where passengers of the California Limited would leave the train to enjoy the food and hospitality of the Harvey House or shop at the Indian Room. Recognizing a celebrity, Dean would approach and ask for a photograph for his collection.

Prominent politicians also often visited the Alvarado. For many years, a large public room in the hotel was known as the Taft Room because President William Howard Taft was welcomed to Albuquerque with an event there. Later, Senator Robert A. Taft, the president's son, visited the Alvarado and enjoyed a meal prepared by Chef Charlie Zuellig, one of the notable Alvarado chefs whose recipe for chicken in sherry and cream was the featured "Dish of the Month" in the June 1952 *Esquire* magazine. Another favorite recipe from Chef Zuellig was Caruso Salad: lettuce, tomatoes and pineapple topped with French dressing.

With the considerable exposure of celebrities and creative individuals to the Alvarado and its Indian Curio Building, the experiences crept into the culture of the time. One example is a scene in the 1940s movie *Rhapsody in Blue*, the fictionalized life story of American composer George Gershwin. During a train trip to California from New York, Gershwin mentions to one of his traveling companions that he (Gershwin) thought they had left the friend in Albuquerque.

Sugar Cane by Thomas Hart Benton, 1943. This menu cover was part of the Eminent Artist Series featuring the work of well-known artists. The menus were used throughout the Fred Harvey system. *Courtesy of Jack Kelly.*

The friend answered, "I did get off to buy some blankets," referring in an offhand way to the availability of Native American goods at the train stop.

To properly accommodate the news of the opening of the Alvarado on May 11, 1902, the *Albuquerque Journal-Democrat* newspaper doubled its normal run to sixteen pages. The event was described as occurring "in a burst of rhetoric, a flow of red carpet and the glow of a myriad of brilliant electric lights." The usual severe news stories were replaced with photographs of the new hotel and elaborate descriptions such as: "the most magnificent wing of the Harvey Houses now in Albuquerque and musically christened the Alvarado." The intention of Albuquerque leaders to build such a hotel "which would attract the wealthier classes to stop in Albuquerque on their travels to the west" had become a reality.

Fifty years later, an *Albuquerque Journal* news article stated that the Alvarado "is basically the same today as when it opened." Manager John D. Garvin stated in 1952 that the only change he knew of was an addition of a new section "toward the front and south of the lobby in 1922." Air conditioning in the public rooms had also been added, but otherwise, "the Alvarado remains the same in atmosphere and policy." In a telephone interview by the newspaper for the news story in 1952, Daggett Harvey (Fred Harvey's grandson) commented from his Chicago office that the Harvey House in Albuquerque "still tries to accommodate the public and the people passing through and to keep the standards of southwestern hospitality as we've had them for fifty years. The Alvarado is one of our most important branches and there has been no significant change in our policy."

During my research for this book, the images of Chef John Frenden became a dazzling symbol of the Fred Harvey image in New Mexico. This tall, handsome German came to America in 1927 and retired in 1973—Fred

Chef John Frenden worked for the Fred Harvey company for over forty years. He was chef at the Alvarado in Albuquerque, New Mexico, and the La Fonda in Santa Fe, New Mexico. *Courtesy of Belen Harvey House Museum Photo Archives.*

Harvey was his only employer in America. He was photographed many times, often with visiting dignitaries or some of the Harvey family, usually with a huge tray of artfully arranged food. In 1962, Frenden and Alvarado pastry chef John Brumitt were featured on the front page of the *Albuquerque Journal* as they finished a six-foot-square cake commemorating the fiftieth anniversary of New Mexico statehood and the twenty-fifth year of the New Mexico State Fair.

Frenden once described Harvey Girls as "beautiful, high-class women. They weren't supposed to date Harvey employees, but they did." Yes, they certainly did, Chef Frenden! In images of John with Harvey House staff, his Harvey Girl wife, Pauline, is usually in the front row. The couple met at the Alvarado, married in 1954 and continued to work for Fred Harvey in various locations until they retired almost twenty years later, in 1973. Pauline shared her memories of the strict Fred Harvey rules for employees in a magazine interview after she retired and recalled her salary of twenty-five cents an hour with tips. She also remembered living at the Alvarado while working there before she married and having to pay ten dollars a month for her room and board.

It was usual business practice for Fred Harvey to hire European chefs. Frenden, a native of Munich, trained at resorts and hotels in Italy, France and Germany. A relative of John's worked for Fred Harvey in the United States as

Chef Frenden (back row, second from the right) and his wife, Pauline (front row, far left), stand with other Alvarado staff members. *Courtesy of Belen Harvey House Museum Photo Archives.*

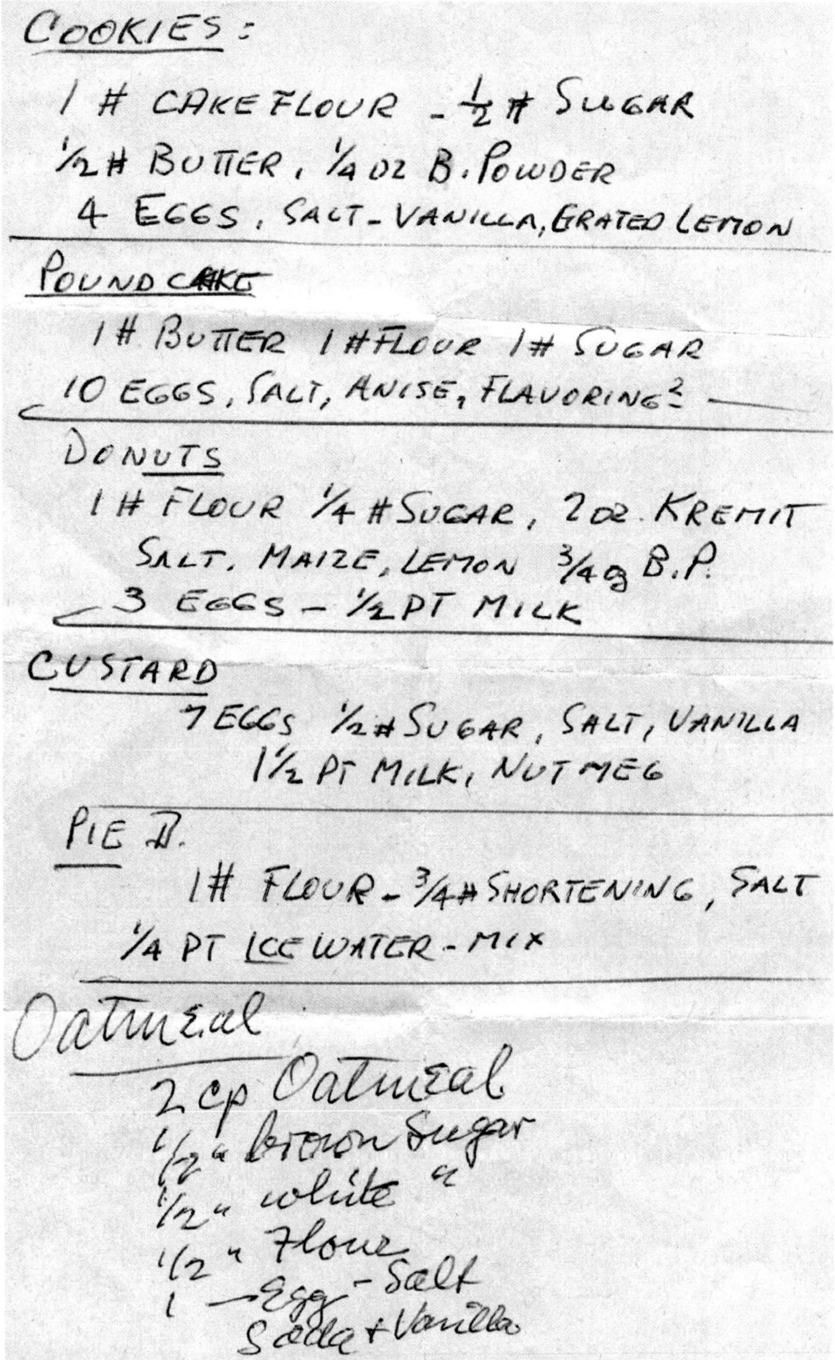

COOKIES:
1 # CAKE FLOUR - ½ # SUGAR
½ # BUTTER, ¼ OZ B. POWDER
4 EGGS, SALT - VANILLA, GRATED LEMON

POUND CAKE
1 # BUTTER 1 # FLOUR 1 # SUGAR
10 EGGS, SALT, ANISE, FLAVORING? -

DONUTS
1 # FLOUR ¼ # SUGAR, 2 OZ. KREMIT
SALT, MAIZE, LEMON ¾ OZ B.P.
3 EGGS - ½ PT MILK

CUSTARD
7 EGGS ½ # SUGAR, SALT, VANILLA
1½ PT MILK, NUTMEG

PIE D.
1 # FLOUR - ¾ # SHORTENING, SALT
¼ PT ICE WATER - MIX

Oatmeal
2 cp Oatmeal
½ " brown Sugar
½ " white "
½ " Flour
1 Egg - Salt
Soda + Vanilla

Recipes used by Harvey Chef John Frenden. *Courtesy of Belen Harvey House Museum.*

a recruiter for cooks, butchers and bakers and assured the young man a job. He was first hired as assistant night chef at Chicago's Union Station and later split his time between Chicago and Cleveland's Union Terminal. In 1951, he was transferred to the Alvarado, where he presided over the kitchen services, and at the La Fonda in Santa Fe until 1962. During his last eleven years of employment with Fred Harvey, John was chef at McDonnell Douglas, one of Fred Harvey's custom food operations in Huntington Beach, California.

In an interview in 1985, the chef remembered that "the Alvarado got the elite of the town. The presidents and doctors and attorneys." However, it was obvious that many knew his work; after he retired, he recalled, "Wherever I go in town, people recognize me, but they don't know my name. They just say, 'Hi, Chef.'"

A poignant illustration of the staff's typical appreciation for their experiences with the Fred Harvey company is a typed letter to Daggett Harvey in Chicago from Alvarado employee Dionisio (Dan) Baca dated September 13, 1957:

> *Dear Daggett:*
>
> *I have been working for Fred Harvey since 1905 when I was 15 years old. During that time I began as a potato peeler and worked up to swing cook. I have worked for you in many different jobs and many different kitchens, except for the few years that I worked for the Santa Fe Railroad. My wife, Anita, has worked about 20 years for Fred Harvey also. She worked in the Alvarado pantry and laundry.*
>
> *I am happy that I worked for Fred Harvey all those years and I will always remember for the rest of my life that it was a good place that I worked for to provide bread for me and my family.*
>
> *When I started working in 1905 at the Alvarado, my first chef was a fine man named Bertha. The last Chef, John Frenden, has been just as good to me as the first one.*
>
> *Tommorow [sic] at 68 years of age, I am retiring and taking my pension. I want to tell you that I have enjoyed every day that I worked for Fred Harvey and I feel sorry that I am leaving but I just want to rest my bones.*
>
> *God bless you and all the staff of Fred Harvey.*

As the new era of train travel brought easterners (as well as many foreigners) west searching for new opportunities, the Alvarado developed as a thriving center for traveling salesmen. Often called a "peddler" or a "drummer," the traveling salesman was also known as a commercial traveler. Over seven thousand people identified themselves with this occupational class when the U.S. Census first listed it in 1870. Thirty years later, two years before the Alvarado was built, that number had increased to over ninety thousand. These commercial travelers made up a sizeable percentage of train passengers.

There's no doubt the smiling Harvey Girls, pleasant surroundings and delicious food helped lift the burden of the traveling salesmen's work; however, Fred Harvey went a step further at the Alvarado. The hotel designated Sample Rooms for salesmen to use to display their wares and meet potential customers. Winning the trust of locals was a challenge for the traveling businessmen, and many were eager to align themselves with the high regard and fine reputation of the Alvarado.

A sign posted by hotel management welcomed commercial travelers by wishing them a stay that "is happy, comfortable and worthwhile. Because our business is dependent upon the same economic factors as is yours, our mutual respect and treatment of one another should lead to a long and friendly association." The Sample Room was available for the twenty-four-hour period between "4:00 p.m. and 4:00 p.m. the following day, or any part thereof." Hours could be extended to 6:00 p.m. "for the purposes of closing and packing," and occupancy after 6:00 p.m. meant another day's rent. The notice also stated that "management will lean slightly in favor of those requesting both sleeping and Sample Room space." Finally, the commercial travelers were reminded of other facilities at the Alvarado that might be of interest: the coffee shop, the main dining room, the cocktail lounge, the barbershop, the beauty parlor, the manicurist, the gift and newsstand, the curio shop and the museum.

This friendly, informal partnership between an accommodating hotel and the hardworking traveling salesmen met a natural end. The progress of mail-order houses like Montgomery Ward and Sears, Roebuck and Company brought catalogue shopping to almost every home in the United States, eliminating the widespread need for traveling salesmen.

Jack Kelly worked as a right-of-way agent and real estate manager for the Santa Fe and spent several years in New Mexico. Jack told me during a telephone interview that his first assignment in 1957 was in Las Vegas in an office adjacent to the Castaneda; however, at this time, it was no longer "run by Harvey people." His job required that he travel throughout New Mexico, and at one time, he worked in the Santa Fe Engineering Office half a block away from the Alvarado. "The Alvarado had favorable rates for rooms and meals. I always stayed there if there was a room." Jack also ate at the lunch counter where Harvey Girls in typical black-and-white uniforms served him. "I loved the Fred Harvey coffee! They sold it in one pound cans and I would take those home so my wife and I could enjoy it. I drink my coffee black, and that coffee had full flavor. It wasn't overwhelming, but had a distinctive flavor that might be more welcome at coffee break when you needed something to sharpen you up. I also loved the fresh morning pastries at the Alvarado lunch counter. I was working hard with lots of physical activity, so I could enjoy them."

Special heavy-roast Fred Harvey coffee was always a favorite of Harvey House customers. The company annual report for 1907 showed 300,000 pounds of coffee were brewed that year. As Mr. Kelly mentioned, Fred Harvey coffee was available to take home. The company marketing encouraged customers to do this by distributing printed instructions for brewing the best coffee: "The secrets of good coffee are that it be 1) made strong enough, 2) served hot enough, 3) brewed correctly, 4) always freshly made and 5) made from good coffee beans." Following these points, specific instructions were given on how to successfully make Fred Harvey coffee at home, whether you prepared drip coffee or percolator coffee or used a glass coffee maker or an automatic coffee maker.

Neva Davis first worked as a Harvey Girl in Texas, moving there from her home in Kansas. As was the custom with Fred Harvey, after her first six months on the job, she was given a round-trip ticket home and a month's vacation. During her vacation, she visited her sister in New Mexico, and someone suggested she might go to work in Albuquerque. "So that's what I did in 1923. I came to the Alvarado hotel. I had my old trunk with me, and the manager said he'd bring it right up on the second floor where there was a dormitory. So I had the job." Neva recalled living two to a room at the Alvarado in a plain room with two single beds and a dresser. "There was hardly space for my old trunk." Neva liked working at the Alvarado coffee shop where things were less strict. "We had to have proper etiquette in the dining room. Miss Jenny was our hostess, and she was very strict." Friendly conversation was allowed in the informal setting of the coffee shop, and customers could ask to be seated at their favorite

Fred Harvey private label coffee was a favorite of Harvey House customers. *Photo by Beau Gentry. Courtesy of Skip Gentry's Fred Harvey Memorabilia Collection.*

Harvey Girl's station. "You earned your money in tips," Neva said. "Nobody got any overtime. In the early days, everybody tipped a dime." She remembered a time when Bob Hope came into the Alvarado alone and ordered a sirloin steak. "He tipped me fifty cents. That was generous. People didn't pay attention to the percentage thing. They tipped you whatever they had."

Neva recalled the camaraderie among Harvey Girls: "We had so much fun living in the dormitory—me and Effie Jenks, Edith Haselton and the rest," she recalled. "Gladys Bronson was studying ballet, and she would try to teach it to everybody up there. Some of the girls would try to imitate the customers, especially the picky ones." Neva married Harry Davis, who worked in the kitchen at the Alvarado. "Being a Harvey Girl was no disgrace. Far from it. I was doing my bit to the best of my ability."

Shirley Phyllis Marie Tyrack graduated from high school in Chicago and married Bob Jansson in 1942, and the couple moved to Albuquerque in 1950, where Shirley accepted a job at the Fred Harvey Kachina Room in the Albuquerque Airport. In typical Harvey Girl fashion, Shirley became a very productive, independent woman who made many contributions to the city she chose as her home. She attended both the University of New Mexico and the College of St. Joseph and also earned her private pilot's license to help her husband with his growing aircraft sales company. While ferrying aircraft for Bob's business, Shirley made numerous solo flights crisscrossing the United States. Later she earned her realtor's and broker's license and was a founding member of the San-Bern Federation of Republican Women. After serving on the zoning board of Paradise Hills, one of the earliest developments on the west side of Albuquerque, Shirley, who lived in the development almost fifty years, was named "Outstanding Citizen of Paradise Hills."

Harvey Girls respected the strict Fred Harvey rules; however, stories continue to surface of circumstances when the rules were bent or ignored. Marie Marquez Smiley is one example, as she revealed in a newspaper interview that she was *almost* fifteen (the required age for employment at that time) when she left the family farm between Jarales and Pueblitos and traveled the forty or so miles to Albuquerque to apply for work at the Alvarado hotel. This was in 1943, when the Harvey Houses were their busiest feeding troop trains.

"I had to go to work. There were three of us children, and I was the one who left home," Marie said. "There was about four of us train girls—they called us something else, too, but it's not nice today." When pressed about this, Marie explained that at this time Harvey Girls were called to work any time a train came in, even in the middle of the night, and they were referred to as "call girls." Marie said, "It didn't mean the same then, you know?"

Even though Marie fudged a little on her age, she readily acknowledged that her year as a Harvey Girl was a strict life but that it taught her many good things. She learned to respect authority, be kind to people and have patience. "The food had to be well served. I learned discipline and to be clean. I worked hard. In those days, you just couldn't work with your hair messed up."

Marie was paid fifty dollars a month and provided room and board. She described the atmosphere in the large room with long tables set aside for the troops: "We'd set the tables and make the coffee. And we'd see that it was clean, and everything was in its place. We fed every one of them the same thing, whether it was bacon and eggs or something else. Then I'd take the coffee and ask who wanted some. By 7 a.m., we were ready to clean up the tables. Usually by 8 o'clock, we'd be done and were back in our rooms and put our dirty uniforms in the hamper." During the afternoons, the Harvey Girls could go back to sleep or "walk downtown on Central if we wanted to." The waitresses were required to be back at the Alvarado by a certain time, and "it was always lights out at 9:30 p.m."

If troop trains arrived in the evening, sometimes the Harvey Girls would dance with the men. "It was OK. Most of the soldiers came in from overseas or from a hospital somewhere. They were ill, and they were tired. They were quite polite and nice. They always told us 'thank you.'"

Marie left the Alvarado when she turned sixteen and moved to be near her parents. She used her Harvey Girl experience to get a job at the Railroad Hotel on First Street in Belen and, in 1945, married Charles Smiley, a railroad telegrapher. Surely among some of the youngest women to be hired as a Harvey Girl, Marie had good memories of her time at the Alvarado. "It was nice for a young girl to work there because there was no nonsense. They looked after us and took good care of us."

Aslaug Helene Schau Warren was born in 1921 to parents who had immigrated to the United States from Norway. Helene lived on the family farm and graduated valedictorian of her class of 1939. An adventurous young woman, Helene learned to drive on the sly when her parents were not around. She would drive in circles in a field on the farm, and in the beginning, when she didn't know how to stop the car, she simply continued driving in circles until the car ran out of gas. In 1942, Helene left a secretarial job in New York City to travel with her family on a six-month trip to the western United States in search of a new home.

Approximately a year after this adventure, Helene took a train to Albuquerque with the intention of enrolling at the University of New Mexico, where she planned to major in geology. Helene took a job as a Harvey Girl at the Alvarado to support herself and pay her college expenses.

The interior of the Mary Colter–designed Indian Building at the Alvarado in Albuquerque, New Mexico. *Courtesy of Michael McMillan.*

Helene graduated from UNM in 1946, completing the four-year curriculum in three years and earning a bachelor of science with distinction with a major in geology. After marrying and having three sons, she worked at several non-scientific jobs and, at the age of forty-two, joined the Laboratory of Anthropology as a volunteer. Soon she became a paid staff member. Helene's work as a geologist and archaeologist led to her being recognized by the Archaeology Society of New Mexico as one of a few "truly scientific minds" to affect southwestern archaeology. "A. Helene Warren enjoyed a remarkably energetic career lending a geological perspective to the analyses of both pottery and stone tools." Helene is an outstanding example of the complexity of the women who worked as Harvey Girls and the lasting impact they had on their communities and the future of New Mexico.

The wages Harvey Girls earned often varied from location to location, ranging from $17.50 per month in the early years to as much as $60.00 per month during the final years Harvey Houses were open. When Harvey House service was stretched beyond a normal staff, and in some cases, the restaurants reopened to serve the troop trains, responsibilities and pay were not as structured. Although Marie Smiley recalls a salary of $50 per month, other young women hired specifically to provide food to the troops were paid $0.35 per hour. These "train girls" wore all-white uniforms with black ties and usually worked twelve hours a day, seven days a week. The quality of food was maintained as much as possible, but rationing often influenced the menu items, and paper plates were used instead of the traditional Harvey china.

One of the longest Harvey Girl careers ended at the Alvarado. Opal Sells Hill brought many years of experience with the Fred Harvey company to her job as cashier in the Alvarado coffee shop in the early 1960s. During a career that spanned forty-five years, Opal worked in ten different Harvey establishments, beginning in the red brick Harvey House in Amarillo, Texas.

As the youngest of seven children, Opal took the responsibility of staying home in the Texas panhandle to care for her invalid mother. After her mother's death, the family was certain that Opal, now in her mid-twenties, had missed her opportunity to find a husband, not an unusual attitude for the time. A charitable uncle paid her tuition to a business college where she received secretarial training. However, Opal soon realized that a career as a stenographer was not for her. A friend suggested that she apply to work at the Harvey House in Amarillo.

"People kind of looked down on a girl for being a waitress in 1924," Opal recalled. "But they didn't when you worked for Fred Harvey." Opal had heard of the Harvey rules that didn't allow makeup and required the young women to always wear clean, crisply ironed uniforms. This behavior came naturally

Visitors to the Alvarado in Albuquerque, New Mexico, enjoy a picnic on the lawn in front of the Fred Harvey Indian Building. *Courtesy of Michael McMillan.*

to this young farm woman, because even in that rural setting, Opal had been expected to maintain a proper appearance. However, the table setting in the farm kitchen that she and her mother had shared was very simple compared to the Harvey House dining room, and their meals were certainly not as elaborate. Opal had never eaten—much less served—a five-course meal.

The possibility of working for Fred Harvey appealed to Opal's sense of propriety, and she looked forward to the opportunity to move to other Harvey Houses down the Santa Fe line. "So I went in to see a manager at the Harvey House in Amarillo. He said to me, 'You're the first girl who has walked in here today who wasn't chewing gum. You look like our type.' He hired me that day, and I began work the next morning. I was real nervous." Harvey Girls wore badges on the top left of their uniform, signifying their seniority at each location. "I started out wearing badge number fourteen," Opal remembered. "By the time I left Amarillo, my badge number was 'one,' and I was training girls."

Three years after her first day in the Harvey House, Opal Sells was leaving the familiar surroundings of the Texas panhandle to work at the Bisonte, a Harvey hotel in Hutchinson, Kansas. Opal's Harvey journey later took her to the elegant English Oak Room in the Cleveland, Ohio Union Terminal, and in 1933, she worked as a Harvey Girl in the tearoom located in the Straus Building at the Chicago World's Fair. In the early 1960s, the staff of the Alvarado coffee shop were presented with a certificate of commendation from Shanley International Corporation for the "World's Finest Service Extended" to their tour group. The recognition was proof that Opal kept her Harvey Girl skills and pride in her work throughout her career with Fred Harvey. "I waited on lots of famous people: Jack Benny, Will Rogers, Jeanette MacDonald. It was a wonderful life. I loved being a Harvey Girl."

You can only imagine the rush of activity in the kitchen and dining room when train passengers poured into the Alvarado to enjoy the now famous Harvey House food. Regardless of the amount of training, accidents did happen. Former Alvarado Harvey Girl Violet Grundman recalled one incident involving another waitress, Elva Ostron, whom Violet described as a "beautiful blonde." The girls collided when each was carrying four plates of goulash. "This made a great mess," Violet said, "and caused lots of laughs." Violet was hired to work at the Alvarado in 1937 after an interview in Kansas City with Alice Steel. "She was very intimidating! She said I was green as grass and naïve."

A Kansas native, Violet became enthralled with Union Station in Kansas City "and the Harvey Girls in their black-and-white uniforms." While attending a Catholic nursing college in Kansas City, she decided she wanted to be a Harvey Girl. "I had decided nursing was not for me, and I needed a job." Violet was assigned to the Alvarado hotel in Albuquerque. "I had $6.35 in my pocket when I got off the train in Albuquerque."

At the age of seventeen, Jean Begley was teaching grades one through eight in a one-room schoolhouse in Missouri. She decided to hire on as a Harvey Girl so she could earn enough money for journalism school at the University of Missouri. However, Jean was sent to Vaughn, New Mexico, and a month later transferred to the Alvarado. Keeping her original goal in mind, she enrolled in the University of New Mexico (UNM) and worked holidays at the Alvarado and summers at Bright Angel Lodge at the Grand Canyon until 1941. After earning a bachelor of arts degree in education that year, Jean was ready to advance her career opportunities, although perhaps not as a teacher. Staying in the transportation industry, Jean joined one of the first classes for Continental Airline stewardesses and, years later, donated her uniform to the Smithsonian Air and Space Museum. She returned to UNM in 1953, and after earning her master's in education, she taught in the Albuquerque Public Schools System for twenty-nine years. After leaving the teaching profession, Jean worked with an international high school student exchange program traveling with student ambassadors around the world.

Harvey Girl Nellie Berg Veley worked at the Belen Harvey House to provide service to the troop trains and then transferred to the Alvarado. At this time at the Alvarado, Harvey Girls bridged the transition from serving train passengers to providing food for airplane passengers. "I worked the night shift, and one of our responsibilities was to pack breakfast for TWA planes."

Hilda Velarde Salas's mother worked as a chambermaid at the Alvarado hotel, and when Hilda celebrated her eighteenth birthday in 1938, she began working there as a Harvey Girl. Hilda is one of the Harvey Girls featured in the 2013 documentary *The Harvey Girls: Opportunity Bound*. In an interview for the *Albuquerque Journal News*, she described her experiences that began with serving the Alvarado staff. Later, she helped serve food from the chuck wagon in the bar and eventually became a full-fledged Harvey Girl. Hilda remembered that, at the time, she was the only Latina working there, but she felt no prejudice. "Everybody was real nice. They didn't think to be prejudiced. I felt that I was important, too." Hilda was paid one dollar per day, with payday occurring once a month.

Hilda's fondest memories come from the time during her Harvey Girl stint when troop trains were stopping regularly at the Albuquerque Harvey restaurant. "There were so many soldiers that we used to set tables outside. They were real nice young men. Hilda recalled that each table would pass

The 120-seat Harvey House dining room at the Alvarado in Albuquerque, New Mexico. *Courtesy of Michael McMillan.*

around a plate to collect tips for the waitresses. "Some left ten to twenty dollars. The other customers would leave maybe fifty cents." When Hilda married, she and her husband moved to California and used the money from her Harvey Girl savings to make a down payment on a house.

In Albuquerque, the Fred Harvey company balanced the decline in passenger train travel at the Alvarado by providing its services to those traveling by airplane. The company operated restaurants and shops at the original municipal airport terminal building beginning in 1949 and continued offering these services in the new terminal that opened in 1965. Facilities operated by Fred Harvey in the new terminal included the Kachina Room restaurant, the Casita de Licores cocktail lounge, the Sunport Coffee Shop and snack bar, the Sun Room banquet room and two retail shops. The company also prepared an average of six hundred meals a day for four airlines.

A newspaper review of the Kachina Room by local businessman Gus Patterson in April 1952 described the food as "out of this world, the atmosphere and surroundings so enchanting it reminded you of some South American romantic capitol. The waitress was very pleasant and charming." Note the review did not mention Harvey Girls. The image of the Harvey Girl began to fade with the mix of uniforms for waitresses at the Fred Harvey airport facilities. The traditional crisp black-and-white uniforms (knee-length at this time) were still required in the snack bar and coffee shop; however, Kachina

Room waitresses wore long full, colorful skirts with white peasant blouses. Efforts were made to stay true to authentic Southwest décor. The interior of the Kachina Dining Room featured large kachinas commissioned by the Fred Harvey company from the Hopi tribe of Arizona.

In a newspaper interview, Billie Miller, who worked at the Alvarado and later at the Harvey-owned Kachina Room, explained, "Fred Harvey was the finest restaurant in Albuquerque. At Fred Harvey, the food was always the best and the costumes were so unusual they were an attraction." Miller further described the uniforms in the Kachina Room as multi-tiered colorful skirts over hoops: "They called us kachina dolls." The skirts required yards and yards of cotton, and most of the Harvey Girls made their own skirts.

The popularity of the Fred Harvey restaurant in Albuquerque easily shifted from the Alvarado to the airport. Celebrities dined at the Kachina Room including Greer Garson, Pat Boone, Frank Sinatra and Dean Martin. In 1962, it was reported several times that Vice President Lyndon Johnson had eaten in the Kachina Room. One Harvey Girl remembered that the staff could easily identify Johnson walking toward the restaurant by his tall frame and big cowboy hat.

When Fred Harvey sold to Amfac in the late 1960s, Opal Sells Hill, a Harvey Girl veteran of forty-five years, recalled, "When Amfac took over Harvey, everyone was told, 'Throw out them Harvey Girl uniforms.' And they did. What a shame." In a sense, Opal felt the Alvarado was thrown away, too.

"In 1970, when they tore down the Alvarado Hotel, I went and watched," Opal said. "Cried and cried. I felt ashamed of myself until I looked around and saw other people doing the same thing."

Former Alvarado Harvey Girl Jean Begley Bluestein ate at the hotel the last day of food service. "It's too bad they let that one get away."

Castaneda

Las Vegas

The Chief way to travel for hotel comfort and relaxation…stop at the Castaneda!
—phrase used by the Santa Fe Railroad to advertise the Super Chief

The railroad rolled into Las Vegas in 1880, and the train station and other railroad development was established a mile east of the town plaza,

A striking view of the Castaneda, a Fred Harvey hotel in Las Vegas, New Mexico. *Courtesy of Michael McMillan.*

Railroad Avenue in Las Vegas, New Mexico, in the late 1800s. The Castaneda is the large building on the right and the Rawlins Building, where the Harvey Girls lived, is the second building on the left. *Library of Congress, Prints & Photographs Division, HABS NM-208.*

creating East Las Vegas. A small Harvey House opened in 1883. In the January 24, 1884 edition of the *Las Vegas Daily Gazette*, it was reported, "Fred Harvey, manager of the railroad eating houses, passed through the city [Las Vegas] last night bound for Deming. He will return to Las Vegas in a few days."

The original Harvey House was replaced by the Castaneda hotel, which was completed on January 1, 1899. The new, luxurious hotel was named for Pedro de Castaneda de Najera, author of the narrative of Coronado's expedition to the Southwest. The building is in the Mission Revival style and originally cost $110,000; furnishings were an additional $30,000. In news stories recounting Fred Harvey activities and staff reassignments, Las Vegas is mentioned in various ways—such as "lunchroom headquarters"—to indicate the prominence of this location in the Fred Harvey operations throughout the system.

Set around a courtyard that opens to the tracks, the Castaneda's large dining room seated 108, and the lunchroom could accommodate over 50. There were thirty-seven guest rooms on the second floor, which were reached via a sweeping staircase visible from the lobby entrance. A Harvey newsstand in the lobby prominently displayed reading material, tobacco products and souvenirs.

In June 1899, Castaneda was the headquarters of the first Rough Riders reunion. "Rough Riders" is the name given to the First United States Volunteer Cavalry during the Spanish-American War. Teddy Roosevelt and many of the Rough Riders stayed at the Castaneda.

Most Harvey Girls who worked at the Castaneda did not live on the premises, as was the custom at most Harvey Houses. Instead, dormitory-like living quarters were provided across the street in the Rawlins House. Built in the same year as the Castaneda by another immigrant from England, William W. Rawlins, the building was planned to be a fourteen-room hotel for the commercial and traveling public. Originally a one-story building, in 1902, a second story was added along with the galvanized iron front stamped with

A current photo of the Castaneda in Las Vegas, New Mexico, shows the hotel as restoration of the 115-year-old building was beginning. This majestic Fred Harvey hotel is set to reopen in 2016. *Author's collection.*

The dining room of the Castaneda Harvey House in Las Vegas, New Mexico, could seat 108. The tables are set with customary Fred Harvey linens, silver, crystal and china. *Courtesy of Michael McMillan.*

A Fred Harvey guest registration card from the Castaneda in Las Vegas, New Mexico. *Author's collection.*

A current photo of the Rawlins Building across Railroad Avenue from the Castaneda in Las Vegas, New Mexico. Most Harvey Girls who worked at the Castaneda lived in this building. *Author's collection.*

rosettes and fleurs-de-lis. That same year, Harvey Girls began living in the rooms upstairs.

Belle Ruthven, a Castaneda Harvey Girl, is described by her granddaughter as being a spirited, adventurous young woman. "Grandma was exposed to the finest state-of-the-art kitchen equipment of that time. Since everything had to be highly organized and efficiently done with everyone working together as a team, she learned valuable restaurant skills which she used later as a restaurant owner herself."

Belle was in her early twenties when she and her sister, Elsie, were Harvey Girls at the Castaneda. Belle's granddaughter, Susanne Rear, donated several pieces of family memorabilia to the Las Vegas Citizens Committee for Historic Preservation in Las Vegas, New Mexico. Among those items was a handwritten letter from Belle to her mother. Written on January 13, 1907, on Castaneda stationery, Belle's poignant words provide a realistic, less idealized look into the life of a Harvey Girl:

> *This is after supper. There has been a good many towns people in for dinner & supper today. We generally have more than the usual run but today we had more than that.*

A Champion Dish Washing Machine used in the Castaneda kitchen in Las Vegas, New Mexico. *Author's collection.*

I have been a little out of sorts today. Nothing seemed to go right. I wished I wasn't here but I am. It isn't very often I get blue.

Elsie is taking a little walk with Jim so I am here alone except for our new roommate Agnes. Her 6 months were up on the 5th but she is waiting to be transferred to the western division & that won't be till [sic] some time the end of this week. How we dislike her. She curses & drinks & is absolutely no good. Is just as selfish as she can be & she has been our roommate almost all the time we have been here so we are glad to see her go. I was very willing to write a letter to the General Manager on the western division for her, she can't do it and Mr. Stein, our general manager said she would have to write one and he took the letter with him with our house manager's signature affixed.

And now about that other juice, we have been away from home so long and then you know it's hard to write things, but just the same I have something to begin on right now. It isn't about myself, but Elsie. I told you about there [sic] caring for each other in my last letter, Jim & E. Well that boy is a good boy with a strong will & good principalls [sic]. He has promised her never to touch liquor nor smoke or swear nor he doesn't either. He is good natured, fine looking & thinks Elsie is all there is. They are both very sincable [sic]. He doesn't spend his money. This is the point—there is going to be a masquerade dance by the towns people Washington's birthday & she kind of wants to go. We don't go to dances. The dining room girls had a little dance one night & we were there & last winter we went to Marie's lodge twice & they danced a little both times, but a public thing I don't like. She may change her mind. I have been talking to her about it. Jim don't dance & don't care much about it but if he should mask you see they wouldn't know him & he might learn & when he has promised so much to Elsie. She ought not to put temptation in his way, ought she.

Of course I don't think any harm would come of it but lots of indecent things are done at masquerades. If you write to her about it don't say much, don't let on that I said anything to you about it. You can bring in dancing & Jim some other way for she knows I have told you about Jim.

This is all for this time.

With love,
Belle

Another letter, from Belle and Elsie's mother in Loveland, Colorado, four months later gives us a view of the other side of the experience:

My dear children,

We received your welcome letters on Tuesday. Well…we have been watching for a letter saying you are coming home and still you have not come. Now I think you better come home don't you?

I wish that there was a way to make them give you your passes. I think they have played a mean trick on you. Now do accept Papa's offer and come home at once. Now another thing. Sew your money in stout muslin bags and sew the bag to the inside of your corsets at the top front. Only save out a little change for what you will need on the way home. You have worked too hard for it to let someone run away with your satchel or pick your pocket. I must close now hoping we will see you next week.

As ever your loving Mother.

The passes mentioned in the letter are free train passes to travel anywhere on the Santa Fe line. The Fred Harvey company gave these to Harvey Girls after the first six months on the job, and usually the young women used the free train ride to go home for a visit. Longtime Harvey employees received Santa Fe train passes to use for vacation time earned.

I don't believe Belle and Elsie responded favorably to their mother's plea to come home, or perhaps they didn't respond as quickly as the anxious mother preferred. A week later, she sent the girls this short note: "My dear children, I

Above: A Castaneda guest room key, a lid from a bottle of Fred Harvey milk and a hand-tinted picture postcard of the Castaneda were part of a recent exhibit at the Las Vegas Citizens Committee for Historic Preservation office in Las Vegas, New Mexico. *Courtesy of Everet Apodaca.*

Left: Ethel Willis was a Harvey Girl in the late 1920s in Las Vegas and Vaughn, New Mexico. *Courtesy of Sandy Whittley.*

am getting up a party to go to the mountains. Now do not disappoint us. Let us know when you will be home…what day and train. Affectionately, Mama."

Ethel Irby Willis was born just sixteen miles northwest of Raton in Brilliant, New Mexico, a tiny mining town. After graduating from high school, Ethel went to work as a Harvey girl at the Castaneda in Las Vegas in 1928 and later transferred to Vaughn. Her daughter, Sandy Whittley, remembers how her mother's Harvey Girl experience stayed with her. "I could see it in my mother's work ethic, in the way she kept herself and her home, the way she folded clothes, polished silver—that dreaded job—and in the way she treated everyone she met. She said it gave her not just a job but a place in the world and a way of life." Sandy recalled a story her mother told her about an experience in Las Vegas:

> *One Christmas she was working in Las Vegas and she was very homesick. It was the first time she had been away from home. She had bought some new shoes that she just had to have. She was out window shopping and it began to rain. Her pretty new shoes were not leather at all and began to fall apart when they got wet. Mother said she didn't believe she had ever felt more lonely in her life, but when her shift time came, off she went to work.*

"It was in Vaughn in 1931 that my mother met my dad while she was working at the Harvey House," Sandy said. Ethel was twenty, and Sumner Irby, a Boston wool buyer, was thirty-five. "To her, he was an old man and it took him over two years to convince her to marry him."

Nina Strong's first sight of the impressive Castaneda lunchroom and dining room was in 1941 when she was a senior in high school in Roy, New Mexico. The school principal brought Nina and another student to Las Vegas to have lunch. The trip of approximately seventy-five miles, plus the experience of spending time at the Castaneda, was quite a treat for the girls. During a recent interview, Nina recalled that the principal "always encouraged her students to go to college after graduation." The principal also knew the manager at the Castaneda and, during this visit, spoke with him about the possibility of hiring Nina and her friend. "You couldn't get hired as a Harvey Girl without a recommendation," Nina explained. "I was delighted to have this opportunity because it meant I could attend the college in Las Vegas."

I asked Nina how her mother felt about her leaving home to work as a Harvey Girl. "She always knew I'd move away. She was a well-educated woman, but because of our situation, she was left to support our family. She always worked hard and knew that it would be important for her daughters to further their education." Nina didn't have waitressing experience but had worked at her hometown newspaper after school and on Saturdays. "I had no idea what a tip was. For a little while, I thought the customers were forgetting some of their money. But, I soon learned!"

As in any Harvey establishment, there was an air of correctness at the Castaneda. "If you did what they taught you, the way they taught you, everything was fine. Chef Victor could be hateful if your order wasn't correct. He would hold the order if you didn't do it right."

Nina lived with two other girls and a dorm mother in a wing off of the kitchen in the Castaneda. "We had the biggest bathtub I ever saw in my life! It was at least eight feet long." Nina enrolled at Highlands University, where she attended school during the day. Her regular Harvey Girl shift was from 10:00 p.m. to 6:00 a.m. "My duty was what we called 'side work.' I would fold napkins, polish furniture and make coffee for the next shift. There was lots of furniture to polish! We used a mixture of black coffee and olive oil." There were few customers during her shift, but if anyone came in, "everything always had to be perfect." Nina walked to the university for her classes and

Top: Chef Victor presided over the kitchen of the Castaneda in Las Vegas, New Mexico, during the 1940s. *Courtesy of Nina Strong.*

Left: Castaneda Harvey Girl Nina Strong is dressed in the all-white uniform traditionally worn to serve Sunday guests. *Courtesy of Nina Strong.*

Former Harvey Girl Nina Strong returned in 2014 to visit the Castaneda in Las Vegas, New Mexico, for the first time since she worked there in the early 1940s. *Author's collection.*

This white china decorated with a dark blue chain design was used at the Castaneda in Las Vegas, New Mexico. *Courtesy of Everet Apodaca.*

remembered that she was never asked to skip class to work. "I didn't have much free time," she said. "On the weekends, I would have time to catch up on my sleep. I slept whenever I could!"

Nina's most memorable experience while working as a Harvey Girl was the attack on Pearl Harbor, December 7, 1941. "My friends woke me up to tell me what had happened," she remembered. "The hotel was in bedlam!" Soon, troop trains began arriving at the Castaneda. "The hotel knew ahead of time when the troops were coming and what we were going to serve. We had thirty minutes to feed them and send them on their way." Even though it was wartime, Nina recalled the quality of food maintained the Harvey standard. "Always the best!"

At the time of our interview in 2014, Nina was ninety-two years old and maintained her own home, lived alone and was still driving. After seventy years, this was her first time back to the Castaneda.

A Castaneda dinner menu in August 1947 included the diner's choice of a steamed filet of Alaskan salmon, parsley sauce, French fried potatoes and a coleslaw salad or boiled smoked ox tongue with a garden spinach, lettuce and tomato salad—either for $0.90. The special dinner that evening was $1.75 and included soup, juice, a melon ball or a fruit cup, a seafood cocktail and a choice of entrée: a sautéed filet of northern halibut, creamed breast of turkey, a roast leg of lamb, a veal steak or cold boiled ham with sardines.

After closing in 1948, the Castaneda was dormant except for the bar, which was opened often enough to validate the state liquor license. A few years ago, the once-majestic Fred Harvey hotel caught, and held, the attention of Allan Affeldt; his wife, Tina Mion; and his partner, Dan Lutzick. After lengthy negotiations, the partners purchased the twenty-five-thousand-square-foot hotel. Shortly after closing the deal, state officials, including Governor Susanna Martinez, joined hundreds of Las Vegas residents and visitors for a celebratory event in the dining room of the hotel. Work to restore the hotel is well underway, but even with renovation in high gear, arrangements were recently made for the filming of a high-profile Netflix TV series at the hotel. Some guest room accommodations will be complete in 2016. There are also local efforts underway to save the former Harvey Girl residence, the Rawlins House, which is still standing but in dreadful condition across the street from the Castaneda.

El Navajo

Gallup

I didn't wake from a nap and missed meeting Elvis!
—Harvey Girl Ella Mae Arthur

The Santa Fe Railroad and the Mother Highway, Route 66, ran parallel through Gallup in the early 1900s. Fred Harvey built El Navajo in 1923 between the two busy thoroughfares, replacing an early Harvey House that had opened in 1895. Designed by Mary Colter, the architecture of the new structure was a departure from the Spanish-influenced design of other Harvey luxury hotels. The name and architecture were a tribute to the Navajo Native Americans whose reservation lay just north of Gallup. Rare Indian sand paintings were focal points in public areas, and Navajo rugs warmed the red tile floors. This spectacular Harvey hotel, El Navajo, at the western edge of the state, was Colter's last project.

Complicated negotiations were required by the Santa Fe Railroad to purchase land for right of way for its westward expansion in the late nineteenth century. This right of way stretched across Laguna Pueblo lands, and the railroad offered a lump sum of money to the tribe to make way for tracks across their land. The tribal leaders refused the money and

The Santa Fe Depot and Fred Harvey El Navajo Hotel in Gallup, New Mexico. *Courtesy of Michael McMillan.*

Fred Harvey architect Mary Colter designed El Navajo in Gallup, New Mexico, and decorated this spacious lobby using authentic Native American art and artifacts. *Courtesy of Michael McMillan.*

asked instead for employment on the railway for the tribal men. Laguna Pueblo men were sent to California, Arizona and Gallup, New Mexico, to work. Boxcars were moved near the tracks to provide housing for the men and their families.

Katherine Augustine's father went to work in the Santa Fe roundhouse in Gallup in 1941, moving her mother and six of her siblings from the pueblo to the box car village. Katherine stayed with her grandmother in Albuquerque and attended the Indian Boarding School. She visited her family in Gallup on summer vacations and worked at El Navajo as a Harvey Girl serving meals to travelers.

An El Navajo menu from August 29, 1946, offered this sandwich selection: a fried egg sandwich, fifteen cents; a peanut butter and jelly sandwich, twenty cents; a sliced chicken sandwich, forty cents; and a chicken salad sandwich, thirty-five cents. You could also order homemade chili for twenty cents or enjoy a chilled tomato stuffed with chicken salad and a boiled egg for fifty cents.

The chef's suggestions for this day were a creamed turkey sandwich on toast au gratin, with snowflake potatoes, sixty-five cents; the El Navajo club sandwich "3 decker," with sliced tomato, ripe olives and dill pickles, seventy-five cents; or the health plate of selected California fruit with cottage cheese and Jello [*sic*], sixty-five cents. A light lunch of tomato soup with rice was available for twenty cents for a bowl or fifteen cents for a cup. Another lunch selection was a fried filet of sole with tartar sauce for seventy-five cents.

Other standard meals—such as homemade pork sausage with mashed potatoes and applesauce or sweetbreads and capon a la King en casserole—were available for seventy-five cents. Diners could finish their meals with their choice of these desserts: two cupcakes, ice cream, pie, pudding or prunes—all ten to fifteen cents per serving.

The El Navajo manager at the time, D.M. Maga, who had also served as manager of the Alvarado in Albuquerque, printed the following statement on the menu regarding the 1946 Famine Emergency Committee program:

> *We, in cooperation with the Famine Emergency Committee program for feeding the starving people of the world, are endeavoring to conserve on the use of oil and wheat. We are required to offer the same portions as during April 4 to 10, 1943. However, the usual second roll, slice of bread, additional crackers, basket or plate of bread or rolls or extra helping of oil salad dressing will be served you only if you request it.*

President Harry S. Truman established the Famine Emergency Committee on March 1, 1946, for the purpose of aiding the fight against world famine. The program was short-lived. A letter from the president to members of the committee, dated November 29, 1946, stated that record grain production during the year made it unlikely that further sacrifices by American consumers and industrial users would be required.

Mary Toki Montoya worked at El Navajo during its glory days and remembers the glamour of the two-story building and the parties. She also recalls the rigid rules and crisp uniforms. Mary came to Gallup at the age of twelve when her Japanese father was hired as a cook at the coal mining camp in Gamerco. She began working at El Navajo as a waitress to the railroad employees at the lunch counter; next she served customers at the counter and then was a waitress in the lunchroom. "Even if you thought you were the best waitress in Gallup, you had a lot to learn," she said. "You started at the bottom." Mary eventually became the head waitress, serving in the main dining room where the place settings included individual finger bowls. During her ten-year Harvey Girl career in Gallup, Mary saw many celebrities, including her favorite, Clark Gable.

At sixteen, Ella Mae Arthur's first job was as a waitress at El Navajo. In addition to her job in Gallup, she also worked in a dining car, riding the

The large dining room at El Navajo in Gallup, New Mexico, could seat over one hundred. *Courtesy of Michael McMillan.*

train from Seligman, Arizona, to Santa Fe, New Mexico, and back. In an interview, Ella Mae revealed one regret during her Harvey Girl days: "I didn't wake from a nap and missed meeting Elvis!"

In earlier years, when most Harvey Girls came west from the northeastern and midwestern parts of the United States, the Fred Harvey company required future Harvey Girls to sign a contract that they would not marry until they had worked at least six months. This agreement would prove to be a challenge as young women moved to remote locations where they were inevitably pursued by local men and railroad men. As the West became more populated and more local women were hired by Harvey managers, new Harvey Girls were not always required to sign such a contract.

According to family memories, Gallup Harvey Girl Daisy Mangum met her husband, Jim Garrison, "across the counter when Jim would stop at the Harvey House for breakfast." Daisy was born in Utah, but her family ended up in New Mexico, where she graduated from high school in 1942. She and Jim, a railroad fireman, married in October of the same year, indicating a short career as a Harvey Girl for Daisy.

Antonia Madrid and her sister, Bernice, both worked at the El Navajo in Gallup. Antonia's employment began in 1941 and continued for nine years. She wrote about her Harvey Girl memories in 2006 in a notebook

El Navajo Harvey House staff in Gallup, New Mexico, circa 1933. *Courtesy of Baumgartner-Leonard Collection.*

that was kept at that time by Maurine McMillan, director of the Belen, New Mexico Harvey House Museum. Antonia described her Harvey Girl uniform as a white wraparound skirt, white blouse and white shoes. "They were very starched. They could stand up by themselves." She also recalled other Gallup Harvey House employees: bellhop Fred Houston and a head waitress from Kansas City who trained the Harvey Girls and was very strict. "Hair nets were required, pencil over ear was not allowed."

Antonia wrote that her most memorable experience was serving the troop trains during World War II. During this time, she was required to stay in the on-site dormitory because the waitresses were called at all hours to feed the troops. "I met my husband in 1948 when he returned from the service and went to work at the El Navajo. He became a great baker. He learned from Mr. Ernie Stangl from Kansas City."

Mildred M. Ludwick was born in 1905 in Kansas—the birthplace of Harvey Houses. She graduated from Emporia State Teachers College and taught school in rural Kansas. Evidently the possibility of a more exciting life appealed to Mildred, for she applied for a job as a Harvey Girl and soon boarded a train to Gallup. She later worked in the Harvey House in Ashfork, Arizona, where she met her husband, Louis, a native of Oklahoma and a timekeeper for the Santa Fe. According to family history, Mildred gave up her Harvey Girl life after the wedding; however, Louis was employed by the Santa Fe for forty-five years.

According to her son, Charles, former Harvey Girl Helene Elizabeth Stout Mitchell was actually named "Helen" when she was born in 1919 in Los Angeles, California, but she never liked the name, so she added an *e* and became Helene. She grew up in Winslow, Arizona; graduated from high school; married; and moved to California. Helene's marriage ended in divorce, and she moved with her two sons back to Arizona to be near her family. While her sons were secure with their grandparents, Helene sought opportunities to help support her family.

For the next few years, Helene's work experience made her a unique part of women's history in the United States. She is one of the few women who worked in a defense aircraft plant and in a Harvey House. Helene was both a Rosie the Riveter *and* a Harvey Girl!

We don't have the details of how this young woman made her way from an aircraft plant in Washington to El Navajo in Gallup, New Mexico, but we do have proof that she was a successful Harvey Girl. Her customers wrote sentiments of appreciation on a restaurant menu and presented it to her on her last day of work in Gallup before moving to Albuquerque. During a time when it was difficult for single young women to find employment that paid well enough to support their families, Harvey Girl wages were at least thirty dollars per month with room and board, and tips often doubled the wages. Usually tips were a dime; however, one Harvey Girl recalls receiving a five-dollar tip from movie star Tom Mix for her good service, and one frequent train passenger who owned silver mines often left a silver ring for his waitress. Usually Harvey Girls working the lunch counter kept their individual tips; however, in the dining room, tips were combined and then split evenly among the women.

In 1949, Helene met and married Howard Mitchell, and during their forty-six-year marriage, the couple enjoyed traveling within the United States and overseas. Helene also became a Red Cross volunteer and received commendation for over one thousand hours of work as a Gray Lady in air force hospitals. She was also very active in the lay ministry of St. Michael and All Angels Episcopal Church in Albuquerque, serving thirty years as a lay reader, chalice bearer, acolyte, lector and a member of both the Altar Guild and the Daughters of the King.

Becoming a Harvey Girl was often viewed as an exciting opportunity for a young woman—it was a safe way to travel and experience life in places you probably would never see otherwise. However, there were times when these employment opportunities met a very practical need. Thelma Drzewiecki was not looking for adventure when she became a Harvey Girl in 1932.

National Guard officers and off-duty Harvey Girls in Gallup, New Mexico, in 1933, at the time of Gamerco coal miners' strike. *Left to right*: Beulah Messer, Chief Lieutenant Morrison, Lydia Schacht, Lieutenant Sam Morgan, Lieutenant Jimmy Sadler and Ethel Reed. *Courtesy of Baumgartner-Leonard Collection.*

At the age of twenty-three, Thelma's husband had died in a construction accident, and she had an eighteen-month-old daughter. Someone suggested she go to the Alvarado to apply to become a Harvey Girl. A "line waitress" could make as much as sixty dollars per month plus room and board.

Thelma had no idea what a line waitress was, but during the interview, she was told that it meant she would be living out of a suitcase from one end of the Santa Fe Railroad to the other, from Chicago to Los Angeles. Thelma was also assured that she would be able to find work anywhere in the world when she had this extensive training and experience. The prospects sounded good, and Thelma became a Harvey Girl. Of course, as promised, the training she received was very thorough. "The silver had to be polished just so, the napkins folded just right, and the seams in your stockings had to be perfectly straight." All the girls had to answer to a matron who was responsible for their work and their living arrangements. "She had full control of those girls…ladies. I mean, we were turned from little street girls to ladies immediately," Thelma said.

Thelma's first job with the Fred Harvey company was in Gallup. "Gallup was wild and rough. We used to call it 'little Chicago,' and it was just that.

Off-duty Harvey Girls posing on the Harvey House roof in Gallup, New Mexico, circa 1933. *Courtesy of Baumgartner-Leonard Collection.*

There were very few Harvey Girls there," she said. The day Thelma arrived in Gallup, a coal miners' strike against the railroad had turned violent. "I saw them beating each other up with clubs. So I turned, and a big man grabbed hold of me and said, 'Kid, if you got a home you find it. Them people's killing each other.'" She escaped injury that night by immediately boarding the bus back to Albuquerque; however, she later returned and worked in Gallup for many of the sixteen years she was a Harvey Girl.

In 1907, when Frieda Baumgartner was one year old, her family immigrated to the United States from Switzerland and settled on a farm in Illinois. As a young woman, Frieda worked as a maid in Lake Geneva,

Wisconsin, and in the famous Elgin watch factory. In the mid- to late 1920s, Frieda and her sister, Hattie, headed west.

Surely the atmosphere in the Gallup Harvey House brightened when Frieda reported for work. Photos from an album she kept show a pretty, fun-loving girl on a New Mexico adventure. Frieda is pictured with co-workers and friends playing in the snow and on excursions far away from the rush of Harvey Girl responsibilities. There are even a few images of off-duty Harvey Girls, posing on the roof of El Navajo in silky lingerie and elegant evening wear.

In 1933, Frieda married Bob Leonard, who was manager of the El Morro Theatre in Gallup. The couple moved to California, and later with their three children settled in Winslow, Arizona, where they owned a business.

Frieda's granddaughter, Patt Leonard, scanned her grandmother's keepsake photos and, in addition to sharing a few for this book, included copies with her family Christmas letter. Patt wrote, "I enjoy looking at these photos because this is the way I remember my grandmother, as a high-spirited woman who worked hard but knew how to have fun."

The former El Navajo structure now houses the Gallup Cultural Center, with a visitors' center, museum and art gallery as well as an Amtrak station. Gallup's population has now surpassed twenty thousand and claims over one hundred trading posts, shops and galleries offering merchandise very similar to what was sold in the original Fred Harvey Indian curio shops.

El Ortiz

Lamy

It was like a private house of someone who had lavished thought and care upon every nook.
—*Owen Wister, author*

The original expansion plans for the Santa Fe Railroad were for the tracks to run from Kansas to Santa Fe, New Mexico, and then proceed west to California. However, the railroad civil engineers determined that the hills surrounding the town of Santa Fe were too steep for the engines of the time. The main railway line was instead built through Lamy, approximately eighteen miles southeast of Santa Fe, and later, a spur line was built into the state capital.

El Ortiz in Lamy, New Mexico, had fewer than a dozen guest rooms, all of which opened onto a courtyard. *Courtesy of Michael McMillan.*

In 1910, the cozy, distinct El Ortiz replaced a Fred Harvey lunchroom that had opened in 1883. Fred Harvey transferred well-respected manager P.J. Crozier from the Gainesville, Texas Harvey House to open the restaurant in the new El Ortiz Harvey hotel.

The small hotel was built in the Pueblo Revival style, designed by renowned architect Louis Curtiss with interior designs by Mary Colter. I am a big fan of Curtiss's work, and to me, the partnership with Colter seems like a perfect match to design an intimate, appealing destination hotel. Of the many well-planned, beautiful Harvey hotels, I'm most intrigued with El Ortiz and its contrast with La Fonda in Santa Fe.

El Ortiz could seat thirty-four at the lunch counter and twelve in the dining room. Some company records show only eight rooms in the "boutique" hotel, while others count eleven. Either way it was a small hotel, especially by Harvey standards. Originally called "Los Pinos," the Santa Fe employee magazine reported the name was changed to honor a historic character, Ortiz, who was "in and about Lamy in the days of the Santa Fe Trail."

A quarter of a century after El Ortiz opened, it was known as "the littlest hotel in the littlest town." At that time, the population of Lamy was just over three hundred. Regularly scheduled Fred Harvey Indian Detours began at El Ortiz and continued to La Fonda in Santa Fe and points beyond. The groups would then be returned to Lamy to continue their journey by train. As interest in the Detours grew, all major Harvey hotels in the Southwest offered the tours.

While I was unable to find individual Harvey Girl experiences at El Ortiz, one account stated that it became known as the Honeymoon Hotel, employing sixty-two young managers between 1910 and 1938. This designation implies the managers married Harvey Girls and moved on to other Harvey locations. Another account states that Lamy was bypassed by younger Harvey Girls because of its remote location, a fact that made it appealing to older Harvey Girls who welcomed the slower pace.

Many scientists involved in the ultra-secret Manhattan Project at Los Alamos, New Mexico, in the mid-1940s traveled by train to Lamy, fifty miles northwest of their final destination, and covered the final leg of their trip by bus or special car. Lamy's significance as a railroad junction and its relation to the project is recounted in the 1980 documentary *The Day After Trinity*. The 1949 movie *Fancy Pants*, starring Bob Hope and Lucille Ball, was filmed in Lamy, and of the dozen or so movies filmed at least partly in this location, the latest is the 2014 movie *The Lone Ranger*, starring Johnny Depp.

The author of *The Virginian*, Owen Wister, didn't write about Lamy in his books; however, he did write a glowing review of his stay at El Ortiz for the Santa Fe employees' magazine, stating, "The temptation was to give up all plans and stay a week for the pleasure of living and resting in such a place." The writer described his "agreeable surprise in finding such a delightful stopping place" where he had expected "an hostelry with the barnlike appearance and conveniences which experience had taught him abounded in the small junction towns of the country." After leaving Lamy on a train headed east, Wister wrote a letter to El Ortiz manager Jacob Stein:

> *When a man is expecting something good and gets it he is a satisfied man. When he is expecting something bad and gets it he keeps cool because he was ready. But when a man has been expecting something bad and gets something very good instead he is not merely satisfied he is exultant and blesses the world and his neighbor and everything that is in sight.*
>
> *Thus it was that I being an overland traveler of twenty live years standing and therefore well acquainted with small railroad junctions, stale beds, old towels, fried meat, curious coffee and no bathroom arrive at Lamy prepared to endure such things with philosophy if without enthusiasm. Instead I found a little gem of architecture, a little clean haven of taste and comfort.*
>
> *But whether by lantern light or by southern sunshine of New Mexico this oasis among the desert hills is a wonder taste [sic] to be looked back upon by the who has stopped there and forward to the traveler who is going to stop there.*

El Ortiz was closed in 1938 when passenger train travel declined to a point that could no longer support this location in the Fred Harvey system. The building was torn down in 1943. Now with a population of one hundred, Lamy is home to poets, artists and musicians. Amtrak operates a station in the Lamy depot, and as of this writing, you can enjoy a good meal at the Legal Tender restaurant in the Lamy Railroad and History Museum. Both operations are staffed by volunteers.

Gran Quivira

Clovis

So many girls, like I was, couldn't afford to travel and see the world. We didn't see the world, but we saw the West and parts of the country we would not have seen.
—Harvey Girl Pearl Ramsey

The plan for the Clovis rail yard and the layout of the town streets was well underway in 1906 when the Santa Fe surveyed the land to establish a division point. A large railroad compound including a Harvey hotel, the Santa Fe depot, administrative offices, a Reading Room and a Santa Fe hospital was complete a year later. The Clovis subdivision was the last on the Santa Fe line to use steam, but the progression to diesel fuel had no effect on

Trackside view of the Santa Fe Depot, Harvey House and Gran Quivira Hotel in Clovis, New Mexico. *Courtesy of Michael McMillan.*

the importance of the division point within the system. Clovis continues as one of the busiest in the Santa Fe system with seventy-five to one hundred trains passing through daily.

Named Gran Quivira for ruins of an Indian pueblo near Mountainair, New Mexico, the Harvey House building is a fine example of Mission Revival–style architecture with an elegant arcade trackside. The following description is printed on a hand-tinted Fred Harvey postcard of the Clovis Harvey hotel:

> *Francisco Vasque de Coronado, a Spaniard, hoping to meet with the same rich fortune that befell Pizzaro in Peru, set out in 1540 in search of Quivira, a fabulously rich city that lay somewhere in the Southwest, but he did not find it.*
>
> *On the expedition Coronado named an Indian ruin "Gran Quivira," which stood near the present site of the city of Clovis. The new, reinforced concrete hotel at Clovis, patterned after the early California Missions, and built by the Santa Fe, is named after this historical ruin.*

Few believed the development of a division point (and town) just nine miles west of Texico, on the Texas–New Mexico border, would be successful and considered it another railroad rumor. The headline of an Amarillo, Texas newspaper just up the line from Clovis declared the idea "a great pipedream." Five years later, Clovis was a railroad center with a monthly payroll of $100,000 and boasted electric lights, water works, sewage, a fire department and paved walks. The town was declared "the star in the east of the new state."

The once-grand hotel, with its grand name, is now owned by BNSF Railway and is in a sad state of disrepair. An article in the March 18, 1920 edition of the *Clovis News* provides a stark contrast between the boom years of the Santa Fe Railroad/Fred Harvey partnership and today:

> *The Santa Fe railroad maintains beautiful grounds around the Harvey House and station in Clovis. Thousands of dollars have been spent in beautifying these grounds. Adjoining this property are about some of the most unsightly buildings and scenes in Clovis. Many visitors who pass through Clovis every day no doubt get the impression that the entire town is composed of just such buildings as are around the grounds near the Harvey House. Clovis needs greater hotel facilities too. A little cooperation along this line might induce the Harvey House people to build a substantial addition to the Gran Quivira here which would help to alleviate the hotel situation.*

Large trackside Fred Harvey newsstand greeted train passengers in Clovis, New Mexico. *Courtesy of Michael McMillan.*

As well as a favorite stop for train passengers, the Gran Quivira was a popular meeting place for state and local dignitaries and organizations. The local newspaper reported in June 1913 that the Cooperative Commercial Clubs met and organized at the Clovis Harvey House. "The banquet given at the Gran Quivira (Harvey House) at least equaled if not surpassed anything of the kind ever attempted in Clovis. The speaking was par excellence and a general feeling of good fellowship prevailed. The visitors numbering fourteen were made to feel at home and they joined the Clovis aggregation in taking up the boosting spirit with vim and vigor."

Perhaps as interesting as the various groups who hosted events at the local Harvey House is the verbiage used in the local newspaper to report special occasions. On the last week of August 1919, "Mr. and Mrs. Jack Wilcox ordered plates laid for twenty-six of their friends at the Harvey House in Clovis." Another banquet was in honor of "Roy Smith and Bailey Stewart, who have but recently returned from France." At another time, "Mrs. Von Almen very charmingly entertained the Thursday Bridge Club at the Harvey House Thursday afternoon. The time was pleasantly spent in playing Bridge, three tables being arranged." The story also related the winners of prizes that included a silver spoon and a hand-painted plate. Whether serving bridge parties or railroad men,

Harvey Girls stayed true to the Fred Harvey philosophy of customer service, as this was a point of pride for all Harvey employees.

Olga Berg came to the Southwest in 1928 from Iowa to work as a Harvey Girl. Her first job was at the Castaneda in Las Vegas, New Mexico, and then she was transferred to the Belen, New Mexico Harvey House. Her younger sister, Nellie, was also a Harvey Girl in Belen. Olga married a Belen Harvey House cook, Pat Lamb, and they moved to Clovis, where Pat worked for the Santa Fe as a brakeman and conductor. Olga worked in the Fred Harvey newsstand. Trackside newsstands were an important amenity for train passengers. A traveler could purchase necessities such as makeup and toothpaste as well as cigarettes and cigars. An interesting variety of national newspapers and magazines as well as postcards and maps were also for sale in every Fred Harvey newsstand.

Typical items on a Gran Quivira restaurant menu were a hamburger for thirty cents and pork chops for seventy-five cents. These prices are consistent with other Harvey House menus of the time, which substantiates the often-told story that food, price and service were standardized throughout the system.

John Ritchie and Gladys Snyder met at the Clovis Harvey House. Eighteen-year-old Gladys had moved to Clovis from Missouri with her family in 1928. Her grandmother was in ill health, and it was recommended that a drier climate would help. Soon after they arrived, Gladys became a Harvey Girl at Gran Quivara.

John also moved to Clovis during this same time for health reasons. He had been living in Arkansas, and doctors thought he had consumption and recommended that he live in a drier climate. John went to work in the Gran Quivira kitchen. After a short courtship, the couple married in December 1930 and immediately moved to Colorado with Gladys's family. Her father opened a café where John and Gladys used their Harvey training as cook and waitress. Unfortunately the new business venture failed, primarily because a long siege of unusually severe weather kept potential customers safe and warm in their homes rather than eating in restaurants. In 1932, John and Gladys moved to Belen and resumed their Harvey House responsibilities for another year until John found work that allowed Gladys to be home with their children. The family moved several times and had more children, and a few years later, John went to work as the head cook in a Harvey House in San Bernadino, California. During approximately ten years, John worked in three different Harvey Houses. A son, Bill, recalled that his father "told me more than once that

Alby Vesly, far right, poses with the Harvey Girl staff in the dining room of Gran Quivira in Clovis, New Mexico. *Courtesy of Louise Reynolds and family.*

it was one of the best learning experiences of his life. He was an excellent cook and always put quality above quantity."

During World War II, sixteen-year-old Edna Ortega was looking for a summer job and saw an ad in the Clovis newspaper for a cashier at the Harvey House. Many years later, when she was eighty-five years old, I enjoyed a visit with Edna during which she shared her experiences.

Edna had some cashier experience at another local restaurant "and so I went to see about the job [at Gran Quivira] and…sure…they gave it to me right away. They didn't ask how old I was. The boys had gone in the service, and they were desperate for help." She soon realized there might be better opportunities than sitting behind the cash register. "I looked around and noticed where the money was. The girls who were waiting tables were getting tips, and I said, 'Heck, I can do that.'"

However, Edna soon learned the high standard of service expected from a Harvey Girl could be difficult to maintain. "We had a head waitress, Ione, and she was in charge of the girls. I guess I wasn't as good as I thought as a waitress, because she gave me a good lecture, and made me cry. But I learned a lot from her." The head waitress gave Edna some advice, "If you want to be a good waitress, if you want those tips, you better work. And use that smile for something."

"I learned the job is all what you make of it," Edna said. "A lot of customers are kind of hard to please, but I would always give them a big smile. At that time, we had colored people come in, and they had to sit in the back."

Edna lived in the employee accommodations in the Harvey House and was paid thirty-one dollars per month. "We had to serve the troops from World War II, and those boys were on their way to fight. We were excited about the whole thing. When you are young, you don't think about those things. Probably most of those boys didn't make it back home."

The Gran Quivira dining room was transformed into a mess hall for the troops. "The trains would come in around two or three in the morning, and we had to serve them breakfast—four to five hundred at a time." She recalled being awakened around 2:00 a.m. by someone walking down the hall shouting, "Troop train! Troop train!" Edna also remembered serving train passengers. "We served a lot of nice people. Families, couples—we hardly ever got any children. There were many businessmen." Harvey Girl uniforms at this time were white wraparound skirts with pockets and a white blouse with a little black bow tie.

"I loved my job. It was a good job, and the others I worked with were nice," Edna said. "I liked it because I wasn't under my mother's thumb." It seems the young girl had a stubborn streak that almost caused her some trouble. Another, older Harvey Girl invited Edna to go to Fort Sumner, sixty miles away, for a dance. "My mother told me I had no business going, but that didn't really matter, because I had to have permission from the Harvey House. I asked the night manager, and he told me I couldn't go because they needed me to work. I hadn't had a day off in a long time, and I thought I deserved a little time off, and I went to the dance anyway."

On Monday morning when Edna returned to work, the manager told her she no longer had a job. "I felt bad but didn't say anything. I thought he was right, and he was the boss. I went home and got some boxes and went back to the Harvey House to pack my things. Someone knocked on the door and in walked Mr. Boch, the main manager." Mr. Boch asked Edna to tell him what had happened, and after she explained, he told her he thought she had learned a lesson. "He told me I could stay if I wanted to, and I didn't have to think long. He gave me my job back!" Edna smiled and said, "I didn't have a good time at the dance anyway."

The constant traffic at the large, bustling division point confirmed that Clovis was an important railroad center. Later, Clovis became a stopover for the Transcontinental Air Transport Company, also known as TAT. With a goal of cutting the time in half that it took to cross the United States, TAT launched a route that included traveling from Los Angeles to Clovis by plane, landing at an airfield west of Clovis, continuing from Clovis to Oklahoma by train, from Oklahoma to Ohio by plane and traveling into New York City by train. Using this travel plan, a coast-to-coast trip would take forty-eight hours. In 1929, Charles Lindbergh, with Amelia Earhart as passenger, flew to Clovis to introduce the new venture. Many TAT travelers enjoyed an elegant meal in the dining room of the Gran Quivira before their train ride to Oklahoma.

Clovis served as a hub for the coast-to-coast TAT air and rail service for about fifteen months. In 1930, TAT merged with Madux Air Lines, Standard Airlines and Western Air Express to form Transcontinental and Western Air, Incorporated, or TWA. The merger led to equipment with longer ranges of flight and safer night flying, eliminating the need for rail travel. TAT service through Clovis was suspended a week after the merger.

Described as "quiet, soft-spoken and terribly in love with his work," Earl Augustus Reynolds was the chef at the Gran Quivira for twenty years. He first took a job with Fred Harvey as a dishwasher in Syracuse, Kansas, when he was sixteen years old. In less than two years, Earl had worked his way up to the position of chef. He was transferred to the Harvey House in Belen, New Mexico. During World War I, he served in the military, cooking for the commander of the 178th Infantry Brigade of the 89th Division and his staff of officers. After the war, Earl was chef and boss of the kitchen at Gran Quivira.

Living in Clovis with his wife and son, the chef confessed that the family didn't eat at home but took most of their meals at the Harvey House. No doubt this was a comfortable situation for the small family, as Mrs. Reynolds—Alby Vesly Reynolds—had once worked as a Harvey Girl at the Gran Quivira. Normal hours for Earl at the Harvey House were from 8:00 a.m. to 1:30 p.m. and from 5:00p.m. to 8:00 p.m., and his presence in the kitchen was required for special events and late trains.

Chef Reynolds supervised six assistants in the Gran Quivira kitchen, which had a reputation for being an organized, quiet work environment even in busiest times. He credited his seasoning as the reason for his success in the kitchen. "I think seasoning is the most important part of cooking," he said. "They say that practice makes perfect, and if that's true, my taste certainly should be perfect by now, if it is ever going to be." The chef seasoned by taste and considered no dish correctly prepared until it suited his taste.

Nearing the time for the Clovis Harvey House to close its doors for good, Earl remembered that, through the years, many diners took the time to go back into the kitchen to compliment him on their meals. "Colonel and Mrs. Lindbergh have eaten my food several times, and each time they praised my cooking to me."

Chef Earl Reynolds (front row, center) and the Harvey House staff at Gran Quivira Harvey Hotel in Clovis, New Mexico. *Courtesy of Louise Reynolds and family.*

Ralph Kendall was a baker for Fred Harvey for thirty years, working sixteen of those years in Clovis. He was responsible for all of the bread, rolls, cakes, pies and other pastries served at the Harvey House and put on the dining cars of trains as they stopped in Clovis. Ralph used a one-hundred-pound sack of flour daily to make tasty desserts. Apple pie was most in demand in the restaurant, followed by peach pie. During the summer months, when there were more travelers stopping in Clovis to eat, Ralph would bake twenty-five four-and-a-half-pound loaves of bread every day. In the winter, he would cut that quantity in half.

Another longtime kitchen worker at the Gran Quivira, Leonardo "Susie" Romero was the pantry girl for fifteen years. Her responsibilities included supervising the preparation of all salads, sandwiches, cold pates and frozen or fruit desserts. Although it wasn't unusual for a woman to be employed to help in a Harvey House kitchen as a salad girl or vegetable girl, Romero's position was usually held by a man who was called the pantry boy.

When the Gran Quivira closed in 1940, the china, silver, crystal and other fine appointments were dispersed to the few Harvey Houses still operating.

Fred Harvey attempted to find openings for employees at other locations, although many found work in Clovis. Susie Romero was hired by Shorty's, a local eatery. The longtime baker, Ralph Kendall, didn't immediately take another job when the Harvey House closed but instead decided to enjoy a much-needed vacation.

Chef Earl Reynolds was hired by the La Vista Drive In and Dining Service in Clovis. The restaurant's advertising referred to Earl as "chef in charge," and certainly his fine reputation brought customers to the La Vista. A month after Earl began work at the La Vista, a local newspaper columnist wrote this endorsement, subtly paying tribute to the chef's twenty years of success at the local Harvey House:

> *Have you ever eaten trout, so perfectly prepared that it melted in your mouth and felt good all the way down? The most succulent fish I've ever enjoyed was the other evening when Chef Earl Reynolds invited me out to La Vista for a trout dinner. Reynolds offered me the recipe but I didn't bother to write it down, for I figured he's been practicing this cooking business for two decades, so how could I ever hope to prepare such a good dish?*

It isn't surprising that Chef Reynolds enticed the newspaperman with a trout dinner. In an interview before the Harvey House closed, the chef listed mountain trout as one of his favorite foods. The chef noted that through the years, fried boneless breast of chicken, prepared in a way he developed, was the favorite entrée of Harvey House customers.

Clovis native Charlyne Sisler shared her train memories in the local newspaper a few years ago: "I was born in Clovis. My father was a telegrapher and came to Clovis in 1917 to work for the Santa Fe Railroad. The Santa Fe Railroad and the men who ran it were the most important and dominant aspect of Clovis when I was a child. I loved watching the coming and going of the trains, plus the social atmosphere of the Gran Quivira or Harvey House, where my mother and father had lived when they first arrived in Clovis."

For fifty years, Charlyne's father was the Clovis Santa Fe telegrapher, which means, for many years, he helped facilitate food orders for the restaurant at Gran Quivira. Conductors would take food orders from passengers on the train and telegraph the information to the depot. The telegraph operator in the depot would relay the meal orders to the Harvey House kitchen, and when passengers were seated in the restaurant, their steaming-hot meals, made to order, were placed before them.

"My husband, Joe, and I unknowingly boarded the last train to Clovis in Chicago on April 30, 1971," Charlyne said. "There were people lined up all along the way, and busloads of children were brought to the stations to see the San Francisco Chief on its final run. I shall never forget the dining car stewards playing 'Taps' on their chimes when they made the lunch and dinner announcements."

Recent developments in Clovis include restoration of a locomotive positioned in front of the depot building. When that work is complete, the engine will be the centerpiece of a Historic Railroad District that includes the Harvey hotel building, the Santa Fe general office building and the depot building.

Currently the train depot houses the Clovis Depot Model Train Museum, and the Gran Quivira is shuttered and shrouded in vines. At any time, if you stop in the parking lot, you can observe the still very energetic train activity at this busy division point.

La Fonda

Santa Fe

The La Fonda was the place to be.
—Harvey Girl Bernette Jarvis

The La Fonda is on the busiest corner of the historic Santa Fe plaza and has been an inn of some sort for more than four hundred years. According to a hotel brochure, "La Fonda sits on the oldest hotel corner in America." As early as 1607, the Spaniards established Santa Fe as a trading center, and an inn, at the exact location where La Fonda sits now, was one of the first businesses created. (The word *fonda* is Spanish for inn.) The early colorful history of the inn includes stories of shootings in the lobby, hangings in the backyard (over a gambling disagreement) and rumors that Billy the Kid once washed dishes in the hotel kitchen and played the piano in the bar.

Although the Atchison, Topeka and Santa Fe rail line had to bypass Santa Fe because of difficult terrain, a spur line, subsidized by the city, joined the main line in Lamy in 1880.

The original inn was demolished in 1919, and plans were put in motion the next year to build a new one. The Santa Fe Railroad acquired the hotel

The Exchange Hotel was the original building on the corner in Santa Fe, New Mexico, where the La Fonda now stands. The building was demolished in 1919, and plans for La Fonda on the plaza began the next year. *Courtesy of Michael McMillan.*

The La Fonda Harvey Hotel on the plaza in Santa Fe, New Mexico, in the late 1920s. *Courtesy of Michael McMillan.*

in 1925 after a citizen-financed initiative failed; the present-day La Fonda was leased to the Fred Harvey company in 1926. Mary Colter supervised the design work during expansion and renovation by Rapp, Rapp and Hendrickson architects. She returned in 1949 to design La Cantinita (now the French Pastry Shop). Colter's influence continues to grace virtually every corner of La Fonda.

The hotel was recently renovated; however, the prevalent rich, warm decor imaginatively highlighted with La Fonda signature art was faithfully

A typical guestroom in the early days of the La Fonda Harvey Hotel on the plaza in Santa Fe, New Mexico. During recent restoration, many pieces of original furniture were purchased to use in the restored Castaneda Hotel in Las Vegas, New Mexico. *Courtesy of Michael McMillan.*

maintained. La Fonda continues to be a vibrant gathering place for locals and visitors. A 1940s description of the hotel as an Indian pueblo with fine Spanish and Mexican furnishing still applies today, although at that time, public space included an Indian Room, a writing room and a Harvey newsstand. The promise that visitors would experience the charm of the past is still true today.

New Harvey Girls who were sent to La Fonda to work would arrive in Lamy and ride a bus into Santa Fe, where they would find themselves in the midst of the energetic, exciting "city different." La Fonda was considered one of the best locations for a Harvey Girl. The hotel and its popular restaurants attracted tourists who tipped well. One Harvey Girl in the 1930s remembered regularly earning more than $300 in tips during a busy month. At that time, the monthly salary was $30 plus room and board. Single Harvey Girls lived two to a room in the basement of the hotel; however, eventually more local women became part of the La Fonda staff, and they were allowed to live in their private homes. Harvey Girls who worked in the lunchroom and dining room wore traditional black-and-white uniforms; waitresses serving guests on the patio wore colorful skirts and peasant blouses often adorned with turquoise and silver jewelry.

A La Fonda food menu from the mid-1940s offered typical Harvey House food at very reasonable prices. For less than two dollars, diners could choose

A drink menu cover at La Fonda in Santa Fe, New Mexico, vividly illustrated by artist and printmaker Willard Clark, who owned a print shop in downtown Santa Fe. *Courtesy of Jack Kelly.*

A drink menu at La Fonda in Santa Fe. *Courtesy of Jack Kelly.*

from a roast leg of veal, oysters and scallops, roast Rocky Mountain turkey or a breast of Guinea chicken with a choice of vegetables, a salad and dessert. The menu stated that "typical Mexican foods" were available on request, and room service was thirty-five cents per person. You could have a glass of wine with your meal for twenty-five cents per glass.

Fred Harvey's "coat rule," requiring male Harvey House patrons to wear a coat if they were eating in the dining room, was eventually relaxed at the La Fonda in Santa Fe. This rule was previously enforced in all Harvey Houses, and the requirement was even challenged in 1921 by the Corporate Commission of the State of Oklahoma. The commission set the rule aside, claiming it showed discrimination among patrons; however, the appellate court ordered this decision overturned, and the coat rule stood. Most Harvey House managers had a few dark coats in various sizes set aside to accommodate a gentleman diner who arrived coatless.

Coat or no coat, locals and visitors alike have gathered at this Fred Harvey/Mary Colter inn for more than three quarters of a century. Scientists who were working on the Manhattan Project in Los Alamos, New Mexico, during World War II frequented La Fonda. According to La Fonda concierge Steve Wimmer, socialite and actress Zsa Zsa Gabor married Conrad Hilton (husband number two of nine) in room 500 of the hotel in 1942. Through the years, local artists hung out in the lobby, and influential individuals would hold court at a table that was commonly known as "their" table. Long after retirement, a group of former Harvey Girls would meet for afternoon coffee, minus the black-and-white uniform of course.

When the Standard Oil heiress and fashion icon Millicent Rodgers, who lived in Taos in the early 1950s, experienced health problems requiring her to be near her Santa Fe physician, she elected to stay in her own room at the La Fonda rather than be admitted to the hospital. These confinements would sometimes last for weeks.

A delightful interview at La Fonda with identical twins Bernette Jarvis and Beverly Ireland revealed what it was like to be a Harvey Girl in Santa Fe in the mid-1950s. The girls left their family in Minnesota soon after high school graduation and moved to Santa Fe. "We just packed our '54 Chevrolet and left," Beverly said. "It nearly killed our daddy, but because there were two of us, we weren't afraid. We had been to New Mexico on vacation and liked the Southwest." The girls intended to spend their short visit with a cousin who was staying in Santa Fe while her family was working at the New Mexico mines. That was sixty years ago!

"We took jobs as waitresses because we didn't think we would stay long," Beverly explained. "We applied at La Fonda thinking it would be a temporary job." Waitressing was a natural choice, as both young women had worked at the Jolly Green Giant factory restaurant in the summers during

Vintage Fred Harvey door hangers are still used to communicate with housekeeping at La Fonda Hotel in Santa Fe. *Author's collection.*

high school. "La Fonda was preparing for the upcoming legislative session, and they needed more help," Beverly said. "Most of the legislators stayed at La Fonda during the sixty-day session."

The sisters were hired to work the breakfast and lunch shifts because they weren't twenty-one and couldn't serve alcohol. They lived near La Fonda and, after walking to work, would change into their uniforms in rooms in the basement that were once home to Harvey Girls. They were required to arrive half an hour early in the morning to roll the silverware in white napkins; waitresses usually were responsible for serving five to seven tables. "Everyone

Twins Bernette Jarvis and Beverly Ireland—former Harvey Girls at the La Fonda in Santa Fe, New Mexico—are shown during a recent visit to the Harvey Girl living quarters in the basement of the hotel. *Author's collection.*

was nice and helpful," Beverly said, referring to co-workers. "I especially remember the baker at the time, Frank Zinn. He was such a neat man!"

Some things were different from the early days at La Fonda. Harvey Girls were no longer required to live at the hotel. The ebb and flow of customers wasn't influenced by the arrival of trains as with trackside Harvey Houses. However, things still had to be done the "Harvey way." Bernette explained, "Everything had to be carried out of the kitchen on a tray, even if it was just a cup of coffee. We weren't allowed to fraternize with the guests, and once we had finished our shift, we couldn't come back to the hotel." New waitresses were trained by shadowing experienced waitresses for several weeks.

Bernette and Beverly, who were known as "Bertie" and "Bobbie" during their early days in Santa Fe, found their new adventure much more exciting

Twin Harvey Girls, Bernette and Beverly, are pictured with unidentified twin guests at the La Fonda in Santa Fe, New Mexico. *Courtesy of Bernette Jarvis and Beverly Ireland.*

than life in Minnesota had been. "The La Fonda was the place to be," Bernette said. "Legislators, writers and artists ate here as well as local businessmen and women and many movie stars were guests in the hotel."

"One day I walked up to a table to take an order and the man turned to look at me and he had the most beautiful blue eyes. My knees went weak!" It turns out the guy with the blue eyes was actor Glenn Ford, and Beverly has never forgotten the experience. "I still remember how I felt. I could hardly do my job the rest of my shift."

The feisty former Harvey Girls shared another movie star story during our lunch. "Bernette's boyfriend"—Glenn Jarvis, who married Bernette soon after this incident—"always had a fancy car, and he would pick us up across the street on the plaza. One evening, we were going to the El Corral Bar way out on the western edge of town, and as we were getting into Glenn's car, Jack Lemmon walked up. He asked where we were going, and after we told him, he decided he would go with us." Beverly explained that the El Corral was not a fancy place, but they went there often, as did many of their friends. "We weren't there very long when Mr. Lemmon went to make a telephone call. When he came back, he told us he had called a cab and was leaving. I guess the club probably wasn't as exciting as a movie star would want. I remember what impressed us the most was that he was going to pay for a cab to come all that way to pick him up!"

Three years after coming to Santa Fe, Bernette married, and even in the progressive 1950s, one of the requirements of being a Harvey Girl was that you had to be single. Beverly continued at La Fonda for another year, when she also married.

Both women continued to live in Santa Fe, raised their children there and owned their own businesses. Now widowed, they have continued to be involved in the community through their volunteer work at a local hospital and Hospice Thrift Store.

Sara Salazar began her Harvey Girl career at La Fonda in 1950. "I trained for two weeks with hostess Mary Fischer. I started working breakfast and lunch because I was underage to serve alcohol." After two years, Sara worked the lunch and dinner shift in La Cantanita with Chef Konrad. "He was absolutely the best chef anywhere, anytime."

Sara is referring to Chef Konrad Allgaier, the influential German chef who joined the Harvey staff at La Fonda in 1930 and, during his many years, introduced items such as Chile Rellenos a la Konrad to the menu. An often-repeated story about the chef tells of a time when the son of Kaiser Wilhelm stayed at La Fonda. He was thrilled to discover Chef Konrad Allgaier, who had cooked for his family in Germany, in the La Fonda kitchen.

Harvey Girls no longer lived in small rooms in the La Fonda basement, but "four of us shared a room with closet space to change from street clothes to Harvey Girl clothing when we came for our shift," Sara said. "Uniforms were cleaned overnight and ready for us the next day."

After working at La Fonda in Santa Fe for over fifteen years, Sara relocated to Albuquerque and worked for the Harvey House at the airport for a few months. "I was the first and only Harvey Girl to wear a sexy Indian costume while working the bar area," she recalled. "Mr. Stewart Harvey met me at the airport and wanted me to work the bar at the Alvarado, where I worked for many years." Sara enjoyed her years with Fred Harvey: "I very much enjoyed meeting important business people, movie stars and politicians. I left the Alvarado a few months before it closed. I recall seeing the Alvarado being torn down and onlookers with tears in their eyes."

When Viola Gomez went to work at La Fonda in 1949, she was twenty-two years old and had some experience as a waitress and hostess at Fuller Lodge in Los Alamos, New Mexico. She had friends working at La Fonda who encouraged her to apply. "I liked working there and made lots of new friends. Most of the Harvey Girls were local," Viola explained during our

Viola Gomez (left) with other La Fonda Harvey Girls in the colorful uniforms worn when serving in La Placita, the outdoor dining area on the patio, and the New Mexican Room, an indoor dining area. *Courtesy of Viola Gomez.*

visit in her home in Santa Fe. "One of the chefs was mean and would try to get fresh with the girls. Once I slapped him, and I thought I would get in trouble with the manager, but instead, the chef was in trouble. The baker was real nice. He made my wedding cake."

Three years after she started at La Fonda, Viola got married. Almost ten years later, Viola's husband, who was a land surveyor, decided to start his own business. The rule requiring Harvey Girls to be single had been abandoned, and Viola returned to La Fonda, where she worked as a waitress and as the hostess on the patio. Her hostess uniform was a white tiered Mexican skirt with a matching white blouse. Viola worked the evening shift, and her husband cared for their daughters, allowing him the opportunity to build his business during the day. "When I first worked at La Fonda, they would have us stand

Viola Gomez, shown here with her brother, on the patio of La Fonda, where she was the hostess for many years. *Courtesy of Viola Gomez.*

in line before our shift started, and the manager would check our uniforms," Viola remembered. "When I went back, they were not as strict. I liked all the people who would come to eat. The opera brought wealthy people in, and they left good tips. There was music and dancing in the Mexican Room. Billy Pallou was the orchestra leader, and his wife was hostess." She also recalled that in the last years of her employment, there were more men than women providing service in La Fonda restaurants. "I was proud to be a Harvey Girl. The salary was OK, but you really depended on tips."

A fellow employee that Viola was especially fond of was Alfonso Alderete, longtime bartender at La Fonda. "He was the nicest man and had a wonderful smile," Viola recalled.

Alderete was well known in Santa Fe and, when he died in 2012, was remembered by former mayor Sam Pick: "I went into La Fonda, and he was there. It was probably a beer. I don't remember. I was so nervous. I was nineteen years old. He was the only black Cuban in Santa Fe then, I'll tell you that." Pick also remembered the bartender's good nature: "He listened, and he had a hearty laugh. Even if the jokes were bad, he laughed." The bartender was known as "a dapper dresser and a consummate professional who took the job of bartender seriously" and knew everyone's favorite drink. "He never showed up without a white shirt [which he ironed himself] and a tie and a red bar jacket," Pick said. "He looked good all the time."

La Fonda Harvey Girls who worked in the dining room are pictured with Mario Alderete, the son of longtime La Fonda bartender, Alfonso Alderete. *Courtesy of Viola Gomez.*

Alfonso and his wife, Mildred, were sponsored in 1946 to come to the United States from Cuba by a New Mexico couple they had met while working at a Cuban resort. Mildred was responsible for the couple's children, and Alfonso started tending bar at La Fonda in 1950. After spending over twenty years at La Fonda, he worked at the original Bull Ring next to the state capitol and at the Palace. His attorney and longtime friend was quoted in Alfonso's obituary: "He has known politicians from all parties, from all walks of life, and treated them all with the same respect and dignity. Nobody was beneath him and nobody was above."

La Fonda remained a Harvey House for over forty years until Sam and Ethel Ball purchased it in 1968. La Fonda Holdings, LLC, acquired the hotel in 2014. At that time, the 180-room hotel had 225 employees.

One of the new investors, Caren Prothro of Dallas, Texas, described the first time she was in the La Fonda with her parents in 1953 and the impression she had of the Harvey Girls of that time: "Going into the cantina with my mother and dad and those great wonderful women with incredible long, black velveteen skirts with sequins on them and those great wonderful white blouses with puffed sleeves. I thought this was something magical."

Montezuma

Las Vegas

First thing you must understand is that the Fred Harvey organization was no greasy spoon.
—*New Mexico Harvey Girl*

Attracted by the popularity of the Montezuma Hot Springs six miles west of Las Vegas, Fred Harvey built his first luxury resort hotel in 1882 to accommodate those who came to enjoy the springs and to entice more to experience the soothing waters. Originally named the Montezuma Hotel, it later became known as Montezuma Castle or the Castle. The sprawling, Queen Anne–style hotel, seven thousand feet above sea level, was the first building in New Mexico to have electric lights and the first with an elevator. The Santa Fe built a spur to the $300,000 hotel and printed advertising brochures touting the Montezuma as "America's great resort for health, pleasure and rest." Local trains connected with the main line in Las Vegas, making the Harvey hotel a convenient halfway stop for transcontinental travelers.

The brochure described the springs as "some forty in number, and vary in temperature from ice cold to boiling hot." The waters were compared in composition to the "famous hot springs of Teplitz, in Austria. Spring waters were captured in a "commodious bath house, where under supervision of a resident physician, every variety of baths is administered by a corps of trained attendants." The baths were considered effective treatment for "rheumatism, gout, blood poison, diseases of the skin, glandular and scrofulous diseases, syphilis, mental exhaustion, debility, nervous affections, spinal troubles, dyspepsia, etc. etc." The mud baths for "efficacy in cases of extreme or chronic ailments are absolutely unrivalled in any other part of the world." These seemingly miracle baths, including attendants and towels, ranged in price from $1.00 for a shampoo to $12.50 for a mud bath for ten. A massage was $0.50 extra. Benefits were further described in the brochure:

Fred Harvey's first luxury resort hotel, the Montezuma, was six miles west of Las Vegas, New Mexico. *Courtesy of Michael McMillan.*

The massive fireplace in the space that was the Montezuma lobby was restored to its original 1886 grandeur. *Author's collection.*

"remedial mineral waters" and "friendly climate" at the Montezuma offered "special comforts to invalids."

Reflecting the popularity of the area as a travel destination, at the time the Montezuma was built, there were ten other hotels in or near Las Vegas, including the Plaza, Grant Central Hotel and the Grand View Hotel. It seems the Fred Harvey hotel was a favorite, as in its peak years of operation, the hotel hosted as many as eighteen thousand guests annually.

Over four hundred guests attended a gala celebrating the Montezuma's opening night. Fred Harvey was the keynote speaker, and the U.S. Army Band from Fort Union provided dance music.

The original building was destroyed in a fire, and the rebuilt hotel was ready for occupancy in 1884. This new building was advertised as being fireproof, and halls were equipped with fire hoses in the event a fire did break out. Unfortunately, the hoses were not long enough to reach the turret of the hotel, which is where the second, equally destructive fire started. Two years later, a third building, with 250 rooms, each designed to take advantage of natural light and fresh mountain air, was ready for guests. At this point, the name of the hotel was changed to "The Phoenix," indicating that the facility had risen from its own ashes. Harvey soon realized that the new name was a reminder to future guests of the hotel's unfortunate history of fires, and the name was changed back to the Montezuma.

Known for the view from its sweeping covered porch, the Montezuma provided guests space for a variety of activities. One description detailed: "exquisitely appointed public parlors and reading, writing, music and dining rooms." Billiard rooms and bowling alleys were available as well as a game of tennis in the plaza. For a time, a miniature zoo was kept on the grounds. Daily rates at the Montezuma in the late 1880s were from three to five dollars.

Fred Harvey went to great lengths to ensure that the best, freshest food was served in his

Milk cans that were used to transport fresh milk from the Fred Harvey dairy near Las Vegas, New Mexico. *Photo by Beau Gentry. Courtesy of Skip Gentry's Fred Harvey Memorabilia Collection.*

South façade of the Montezuma hotel, which is now home to the American campus of the Armand Hammer United World College. *Author's collection.*

South façade of the Montezuma hotel in 1976. Great care has been given to restoration efforts through the years to preserve the original design of the building. *Courtesy of Library of Congress.*

The dining room at the Montezuma looks almost identical to the way it did in the late 1800s except for the addition of Dale Chihuly blown-glass chandeliers. *Author's collection.*

restaurants. In some locations, this might require shipping food to the Harvey Houses by train, or local food was purchased if it met with the Harvey standards. Such measures were not necessary at the Montezuma, as a supply of many foods was available adjacent to the hotel grounds. The Montezuma Farm grew fruits and vegetables, and the Montezuma herd supplied milk, cream and butter, as well as poultry.

One account claims that Harvey even made arrangements for the Yaqui Indians to bring live green turtles to the hotel, where they were kept in the pools until turtle soup was a menu item in the Montezuma restaurant.

A Sunday menu in 1883, when J.M. Barr was the restaurant manager, did not offer turtle soup; however, Steamed Terrapin aux Champignons was featured, accompanied by French peas, orange salad and cream fritters. Guests could choose from other entrées, including boiled salmon and lobster in butter sauce, broiled leg of mutton or roast prime beef with Yorkshire pudding. Vegetables offered were baked tomatoes, fried parsnips, cauliflower and artichokes "au cream." Desserts included raspberry meringue or lemon soufflé pie, assorted fancy cakes, chocolate éclairs and pineapple ice cream. Diners could choose healthier options to complete their meals, as a variety of fruits was also available: watermelon, plums, figs, pears, apples and oranges.

Anyone familiar with Harvey House history knows that the Depression of the 1930s was the harbinger of the closing of many Harvey establishments. However, it was the national depression of the 1890s that largely brought about the economic demise of the Montezuma. From 1893 until 1903, the resort was only open for summer guests, and it closed permanently in 1903. In the years that followed, the site experienced name changes and repurposing. In the 1920s, the facility housed a small Baptist college before it was sold to the Catholic Church.

A undated letter written by Manager J.C. Dance on "Montezuma College" letterhead describes the hotel and summer resort in Montezuma, New Mexico, as an ideal place to vacation. The letter is part of a brochure describing amenities and explains that it was impractical to keep the college open during the summer. "So to keep this charming place alive in the hearts of the people of the South, arrangements have been made whereby the college buildings will be opened for the summer as a hotel and camp." Rooms with a bath were $1.50 per day; rooms without bath $0.75. Meals were $0.50 each, $1.25 per day and $30.00 for a month. Bathing in the hot springs and pool was free.

The Montezuma was a Jesuit seminary until 1972, and then for almost a decade, the once dignified hotel and grounds were vacant and dilapidated. "When the Montezuma sat abandoned, the windows were broken and you could just go in and look around," Everet Apodaca, a lifetime Las Vegas resident, recalled. "I was in junior high school and we would go to the hot springs and then go up to the building and look around." Apadoca explained that the youngsters didn't do anything wrong, "We just looked around. Some thought it was haunted. I was completely fascinated because even in the dirt and rubble you could see the grandeur. I was fascinated with Montezuma Castle!"

In 1981, the Armand Hammer Foundation bought the property and established the American campus of the United World College there. The London-based institution has twelve campuses worldwide. The facility provides a limited schedule for public tours.

The hot springs are still accessible just off Route 65 north of the college. There are no attendants and no fees.

Chapter 3

SHORT STOPS

Trackside Hotels

Deming

The customers used to rush in so fast from the train that I was afraid I couldn't handle them.
—Deming Harvey Girl Leafy Bond Bryant

A train depot where two or more separate railway companies share the tracks and facilities is known as a union station. One usually pictures a union station in a large metropolitan city with a constant flow of passengers; however, in the southern New Mexico town of Deming, the junction of the Southern Pacific and Santa Fe established that depot as a union station. In the train station building, the Santa Fe Railroad occupied the east end, with Southern Pacific on the west end. A Harvey House hotel, lunchroom and dining room opened in 1881 and stood in the middle, two-story section of the building. Harvey Girls lived on the second floor.

Leafy Bond Bryant was born in Deming in 1896, and two years later, her family traveled by covered wagon to Oregon. After spending time in Texas and South Dakota, when Leafy was twenty-nine years old, she returned to Deming. Before hearing about employment possibilities at the Deming Harvey House, Leafy offered to work for free for a local Chinese café so she could learn the trade of waitressing. At this time, a friend of hers who was a housekeeper at the Harvey House suggested that Leafy apply for work there.

Union Station in Deming, New Mexico, where the silver spike joined the Atchison, Topeka and Santa Fe from the east with the Southern Pacific from the west. *Courtesy of Michael McMillan.*

"So I got up the courage and went and inquired about it. I was accepted," Bryant wrote in a 1994 letter. "Being a Harvey Girl takes nerve and courage." At the time, Leafy was married and had two daughters. Her experience confirms my theory that the many strict Fred Harvey rules were enforced, or not, depending on local circumstances and how badly a manager needed waitress help. Leafy earned thirty-five dollars a month plus tips: "Not bad for a girl off the farm to learn a business of her own," she said. "We had to make a nice spread with the food on a marble counter. We wanted the guests to feel like aristocrats. The customers used to rush in so fast from the train that I was afraid I couldn't handle them. They had to catch the train, and I was afraid they would miss it."

Leafy's circumstances changed soon after she went to work at the Harvey House. Her husband left to visit his mother in another state and never returned. She was then especially grateful for her secure job as a Harvey Girl and continued to work there for two years. Leafy described the Deming Harvey House: "We always had good crowds and a lot of fun. The price was a little higher but still within reason. None of the waitresses ever left their shift without tips." Leafy left Deming and went to California. "I never had trouble finding a job when employers found out I had been trained as a Harvey Girl."

Claud Sheats, who was a manager with Fred Harvey for over forty years, shared many of his Harvey House experiences in the employee newsletter *Hospitality.* "I almost got fired in Deming, New Mexico, over thirty years ago because I took the Japanese bartender and the Polish bus boy out on a snipe hunt and we didn't get back until noon the next day." Claud's career with Fred

Harvey was spent managing newsstands or the Indian curio shops. He spoke the Navajo Indian language fluently and was placed in charge of the Fred Harvey Indian village at the 1915 Panama-Pacific exposition in San Francisco, as well as the Indian village at El Tovar, a Harvey hotel at the Grand Canyon.

Most likely, the most notorious Harvey Girl worked in Deming. Mildred Fantetti Clark Cusey was born in 1906 in Kentucky and was orphaned at the age of twelve when her parents died during a flu epidemic. When her sister Florence contracted tuberculosis, Mildred moved

Harvey Girl Leafy Bond Bryant in Deming, New Mexico. *Courtesy of Luna County Historical Society.*

with her to Deming, where her sister was admitted to the Holy Cross Sanatorium at Camp Cody. Mildred was hired as a Harvey Girl through the recommendation of a friend with whom she attended church.

One version of what happened after Mildred became a Harvey Girl is that she was transferred to Needles, California, and because of the extremely hot climate, she quit and returned to New Mexico but not to the Harvey House. Instead, Mildred went to work at a brothel in Silver City, New Mexico. In the 1930s, while still in her twenties, Mildred owned three brothels in Silver City, one in Deming, one in Lordsburg and one in Laramie, Wyoming. Eventually her "business establishments" stretched from New Mexico to Alaska.

Another account of Mildred Cusey's story claims she couldn't make enough money as a Harvey Girl to meet the demands of caring for her sister and had to make a different career choice. Regardless of the why of Mildred's story, she later became known as Madam Millie and proved to be a very successful business woman. In addition to the many brothels, she also owned a ranch, restaurants and various homes. Mildred was very active in business and local charities and was once described by a Deming resident as "the most sincere and giving person I ever met."

The author of her biography, Max Evans, reported that when Mildred died in 1993 at the age of eighty-seven, "it was difficult to find enough friends for pallbearers." While further researching this unusual Harvey Girl story, I discovered that Madame Millie's last husband of twenty years was James Wendell Cusey, a naval veteran of World War II, and Millie is buried in Fort Bayard National Cemetery. While not entirely living up to the wholesome image of a Harvey Girl, Madame Millie was a survivor and certainly made her own place in history.

A more conventional Fred Harvey story is proof that even when the West was no longer a "womanless" territory, Harvey Girls were most often considered the kind of women men wanted to marry and take home to meet their mothers.

Emma Pavel was born in Texas in 1895 and, at the age of eighteen, traveled to Chicago to work as a governess for the daughters of Bohuir Kryl, the bandmaster of John Philip Sousa's band. Unhappy with her responsibilities as governess, Emma took a job at the Blackstone Hotel in Chicago, where she met Clara Johnson, who would become a lifelong friend. The young women saw ads posted by the Fred Harvey company for young women to go west to work, and as it seems Emma and Clara both possessed the sense of adventure and bravado that was common in Harvey Girls, the young women went to the employment office in Chicago for an interview. Emma and Clara both passed Fred Harvey muster and were sent to Deming for their first experience as Harvey Girls; later, they transferred to San Diego, California.

One of Emma's memorable experiences as a Harvey Girl was a time when she was carrying a tray loaded with food and slipped. When she fell to the floor, plates of food flew everywhere. Later she was told that the boss wanted to see her, and Emma was sure she was going to be fired. Defiantly, Emma entered the manager's office and said, "I quit!" Her boss was surprised, as he had only wanted to be sure she had not injured herself. Emma kept her job.

The Deming Harvey House was torn down in 1930 after passenger train travel could no longer support the restaurant and hotel. The depot was later acquired by the City of Deming, and at the request of the railroad, the building was moved away from the tracks.

The Deming Luna Mimbres Museum, housed in the historic Deming Armory and Customs House, features a Harvey House exhibit in the Transportation Annex of the museum.

Vaughn

*I was very thankful for the opportunity that Fred Harvey gave me. I just think
that people can do anything they put their minds to.*
—Harvey Girl Jean Begley Bluestein

Even today, Vaughn is a remote town sitting approximately halfway between
Santa Fe and Roswell; one can only imagine how isolated this Harvey
House location felt to Harvey Girls sent there to work in the early 1900s.
Actually, Vaughn probably looked very much like Sandrock, New Mexico,
the fictitious setting of the 1946 Harvey Girl movie, although the movie was
not filmed on location. Instead, the entire movie was shot on the back lot at
MGM in Culver City, California.

The Mission Revival–style Harvey House was named Los Chavez after
the prominent Chavez family, who came to the New Mexico territory in
the sixteenth century. This building was finished in 1910, replacing a small
Harvey House that opened in 1883. In addition to the traditional lunch room
and dining room, the Vaughn Harvey House had fewer than a dozen guest
rooms that were regularly occupied by Harvey Girls and local schoolteachers.
Contrary to the implication of its imposing name, Los Chavez was not a Fred
Harvey destination hotel, and except for unusual circumstances, such as bad
weather or train delays, train passengers did not often stay overnight.

A trackside view of the Santa Fe Depot and Las Chavez Harvey House in Vaughn, New
Mexico. *Courtesy of Michael McMillan.*

A group of Kansas musicians stopped in Vaughn in 1916, and an account of their visit described the lunchroom as "supplying the traveler's needs" but noted the dining room was not yet complete. After the concert in the Santa Fe Reading Room, however, "the pleased audience danced on the cement floor of the new dining room" and the Harvey House manager, Mr. Hollinsworth, hosted a banquet for the musicians. One musician's description of his experience in Vaughn paints a vivid image of the remote Harvey House location: "All day Saturday the wind at Vaughn was exceeding the speed limit, sand peppering one's face with stinging effect."

Molly Johnson lived with her family on a farm in Texas, and in 1926, a drought destroyed the crop, leaving the family desperate for money. A relative who worked for the Fred Harvey company in Oklahoma had told Molly's father that a Harvey House was a good place for a young woman to work. Molly's father took her to the nearest Harvey House—which was in Slaton, Texas, fifty-five miles from their farm—and spoke with the manager, who agreed to hire Molly. The plan was for sixteen-year-old Molly to send her monthly pay of thirty dollars home to help her family. After almost a year in Slaton, Molly was transferred to Vaughn, New Mexico, where she continued to work the night shift so she could attend high school during the day. However, romance prevented Molly from graduating, as she fell in love with one of the Vaughn Harvey House cooks and quit both school and her job to get married.

"Clyde Jordan was the cook in the kitchen. Well, I didn't pay attention to him when I first went to work there because we weren't supposed to, you know. We weren't supposed to flirt with anybody, but he put his eye on me." Molly found it hard to ignore Clyde: "When I would start back there, he would throw a pot lid at me or something." The couple never officially dated since it was against the rules, but working together on the night shift, they got to know each other. Molly was still cautious: "I didn't even like him. He was too fresh, too forward. My mother said to just always watch that kind, you know. He wanted to be friends with me and I didn't. I just wanted to learn how to be a waitress." Eventually Clyde won Molly's heart, and because at the time Harvey employees could not be married, the couple left Vaughn and moved to Oklahoma to farm.

Molly's experience with the Fred Harvey company at the time of her transfer to New Mexico underscores once again that the Harvey House staff treated one another like family. Before leaving for her new assignment in Vaughn, Molly was given some time off to visit her family. While at home, she was exposed to smallpox but showed no symptoms of the disease. Molly

This is a portion of the 1,600-foot drop in elevation coming out of the mountains on the Santa Fe line between Belen and Vaughn, New Mexico. *Library of Congress, Prints & Photographs Division, FSA/OWI Collection.*

boarded the train for Vaughn and realized by the time she arrived that she was very sick. The manager arranged for her to have a private room, and she received treatment from the company doctor. Everyone helped nurse Molly back to health, and she was able to return to her Harvey Girl responsibilities.

Elisa Garnas was born in Pluzna, Austria-Hungary, in 1909, and when she was two years old, her family moved to New Mexico, where her father was working in a coal mine owned by a German company. Elisa attended school in Albuquerque but had to quit before finishing high school and found work as a maid to help support her family. One of her employers suggested that Elisa apply to be a Harvey Girl, as that job would offer more opportunities for the bright young girl. At the age of seventeen, Elisa began working at the Los Chavez in Vaughn, New Mexico. "I loved Vaughn and my job," she said. "I was respected and protected, and the management of the house was wonderful." She remembered the commotion among Los Chavez Harvey Girls when Charles Lindbergh was forced to land his plane near Vaughn because of engine failure. "Some of the girls would argue over who would wait on Mr. Lindbergh, but I avoided those disputes. We were taught to treat every customer with respect and provide good service." Because of her demonstration of professionalism, Elisa was chosen by the manager to wait on Lindbergh during his stay in Vaughn, and she even had her photograph taken standing next to his stranded airplane.

Vaughn was a remote Harvey Girl post, and the work was arduous as trains stopped every day, morning, noon and evening, but Elisa enjoyed working there. Admitting it wasn't for everyone, she enjoyed hiking the wide plains and picnicking in the sand hills with other Harvey Girls.

When Elisa's father died, she returned to Albuquerque to be with her family and eventually returned to work as a Harvey Girl in Belen, New Mexico. It was there, in 1929, that she married a railroad man, bringing her career with Fred Harvey to an end. In 1971, Elisa became a United States citizen and changed her name to Elizabeth Alice Garnas.

Fannie Belle Green was born in Texas, but her family moved to Indian Territory in 1899 where home was a half-dugout on the flat prairie. In the early 1900s, her father relocated the family to another remote place: Encino, New Mexico, approximately fifteen miles from Vaughn. A friend of the family who worked as a railroad agent at Vaughn convinced Fannie, her sister and a cousin to become Harvey Girls.

The responsibilities were demanding, but Fannie appreciated the dormitory-style living quarters on the second floor, and she was accustomed to hard work. Actually, you might say she began training for this job at a very young age. When Fannie was seven years old, her mother became very ill, and Fannie cooked and served her first meal to men who were helping with the harvest. Of course, at the Harvey House, there was a chef and kitchen staff to handle food preparation, but Harvey Girls were responsible for keeping Harvey coffee freshly made. The women had to memorize orders and pass them on to the cooks who committed them to memory and rang a bell when the food was ready. A notepad kept in an apron pocket was used only to total the cost of each meal for the cashier. This manner of handling food orders was dropped sometime during the late 1930s or early 1940s when Harvey Girls were allowed to write down a customer's order.

In 1912, Fannie was transferred to Slaton, Texas, to help establish the new Harvey House location there. She and Joe Teague Jr., the night ticket agent, met when Fannie was walking across the brick promenade to the Reading Room after her evening shift, and Joe was coming to work. They married in 1915 and continued to live in Slaton, where they established the Teague Confectionery, a family business that continued for over seventy years.

Jean Begley Bluestein had grown up on a strawberry farm in Missouri and, after graduating from high school, taught school in a one-room country schoolhouse. However, Jean had her sights on more: she wanted a college education, and she wanted to see the world. After four years of teaching, Jean was accepted to a Missouri university, where she planned to study journalism. However, before Jean could begin classes in the fall, she would need a summer job. Jean explained during a 2005 presentation at the Belen Harvey House Museum, "I wrote to the Department of the Interior and asked about summer employment. And the nearest place they knew of was Fred Harvey's place in Kansas City." Still living in Missouri, this seemed like a good possibility, so Jean went to Kansas City and interviewed for a job. "And they said, 'Well, OK, we'll send you to New Mexico,'" and Jean went to Vaughn to become a Harvey Girl. "I think I had twenty dollars in my purse when I got there."

The job was difficult, the standards were high and Jean had trouble keeping up. "Here I am in Vaughn, New Mexico, and the head waitress caught every mistake I made," Jean said. "And I made a lot of them." She soon caught on to the many Fred Harvey rules of service, and when the summer was over, she decided she couldn't leave New Mexico. "I had fallen in love with the atmosphere and the languages spoken by people here, so I didn't go back to the university in Missouri, and I lost all my credits."

A Harvey House manager learned of Bluestein's desire to attend college and facilitated a transfer for her to Albuquerque. While working at the Alvarado there on weekends, Jean took college courses and worked at several other jobs as well.

In the summer, Jean worked at a Fred Harvey restaurant at the Grand Canyon. Always exhibiting an adventuresome spirit, when coincidence brought her in contact with pilots from Continental Airlines, Jean decided that, rather than teach, she wanted to be an airline hostess. "I had decided I just wanted to be an airline hostess more than anything else so I could see the world and enjoy flying." During her interview with Continental Airlines, her Harvey Girl experience was noted. "They said, 'Well, if you're good enough for Fred Harvey, you're good enough for us.' And I got the job!"

Chapter 4

GOOD EATS

Harvey House Restaurants

Belen

You worked your tail feathers off, but it was fun.
—Harvey Girl Irene Armstrong

Built in what had become the familiar Mission Revival style of Santa Fe/Fred Harvey structures, several sources report that the Belen Harvey House cost $25,800 in 1907. However, information obtained from Maurine McMillan, emeritus director of the Belen Harvey House Museum, indicates that trains with passengers did not run through Belen until 1910. This fact was also reported in some newspaper articles. While I cannot account for this particular variation in information, I know that, in some situations, when the Harvey House and train depot occupied the same building, the opening date for both was often recorded as the same date. In reality, completion of the interior of the Harvey House might take longer, delaying the date when food service actually began.

On the ground floor of this Harvey House, forty-five high-backed stools surrounded the lunchroom counter; the dining room comfortably served sixty-four; and the newsstand was brimming with newspapers, cigars and popular Fred Harvey picture postcards. The rooms on the second floor were home to the Harvey Girls and the Harvey House manager and his family. A brochure printed in 1915 described the ground floor as having a newsstand

The Harvey House in Belen, New Mexico. The building has been preserved and houses the Belen Harvey House Museum. *Courtesy of Michael McMillan.*

with the cashier's office, a lunchroom with a marble lunch counter and a "first-class dining room, which featured an extensive menu and fine linen, crystal and silver."

The description in the brochure paints a striking image of the restaurant: "Swinging double-leaf wood doors connected the lunchroom to the kitchen. Oak wainscoting decorated the lunchroom and the dining room walls, and stained-glass panels graced the window transoms. The dining room floor was oak; the lunchroom floor was octagonal tile."

The Santa Fe Railroad first arrived in Belen in 1880, but for many years, because the main rail line ran west from Albuquerque, there was very little train traffic through Belen. This all changed in the early 1900s, when the Belen cut-off was established, and train traffic increased significantly, giving Belen the designation "Hub City."

For many years, the Harvey House was a center of activity in Belen. Trackside Isleta Indians sold pottery to tourists, and locals often came to the Harvey House to see who might be coming and going on the next train. Movie stars Gene Autry and Tom Mix were spotted on the Belen platform. Local residents were regular customers at the Harvey House, and organizations often hosted special events in the dining room.

During filming for the 2013 documentary *The Harvey Girls: Opportunity Bound* at the Belen Harvey House, former Harvey Girl Irene Armstrong offered this description of her experience: "You worked your tail feathers off, but it was fun." Billie Miller, a Harvey Girl for twenty years, added, "You had to be half an Amazon to carry those trays, but I loved it. I used to say I was married to Fred Harvey."

Armstrong answered an ad in the Kansas City paper when she was seventeen years old. "It was in the middle of the depression. I had a job that paid $3.00 a week and it cost $2.50 for a room. Fred Harvey paid $27.50 a month, room and board and your uniforms." She recalls that the aunt and uncle who raised her "knew what the Harvey system was like, so they didn't object" to her becoming a Harvey Girl. "I imagine they were glad to get rid of me!" Irene worked eight hours, six to seven days a week and was provided six to eight uniforms. According to her memories, the story portrayed in the Harvey Girl movie was authentic. "The town girls didn't like us very well because it was considered quite nice to be able to date a Harvey Girl." (In the movie, the Harvey Girls were not treated well by the local dance hall girls.) Irene's Harvey Girl career lasted "about four years total and then I married a railroad man."

Exhibit in the Harvey House Museum in Belen, New Mexico, honoring longtime cook Joe Tafoya. *Author's collection.*

An exhibit in the Belen Harvey House Museum pays tribute to longtime Harvey House cook Joe Tafoya. Described as a "superb cook," Joe began his railroad career with the Santa Fe Railway in Vaughn, New Mexico. Six years later, in 1926, he started work at the Belen Harvey House and worked in the kitchen there until it closed. Joe went back to work for the Santa Fe where he remained until he retired.

Emma Torres wrote her Harvey Girl memories in the Belen museum Red Log Book. She and her sister Maria "Molly" Gaboldon lived on the second floor of the Harvey House from 1943 to 1945. Molly's responsibilities were in the kitchen making salads, and Emma was a waitress. "I worked in the Troop Room. We used to feed hundreds of men when they came in on the train. We would start feeding them at 5 a.m."

Another young woman who survived the scrutiny of Fred Harvey interviewer Alice Steel in Kansas City was Hannah Bryant McConnel. Hannah described herself as a "country girl from Sedalia, Missouri." Hannah had a "beauty" license, and a friend suggested they apply at the Fred Harvey company. "I was hired immediately and sent to Belen." She worked in Belen for six months, left and then came back to New Mexico to marry a Santa Fe Railroad conductor, Gordon McConnel.

Belen Harvey Girl Nellie Berg Veley described the strong bond between Harvey and Santa Fe employees. "The railroad men were always our friends. I had just used my vacation to go back home to Iowa as my father was quite ill." Not long after returning to Belen from her time off, Nellie's father grew worse. "I knew I couldn't afford to go back home again. As I went on duty, a railroad man approached me with a gift—a round-trip bus ticket and some cash from the railroad men. I cried. They sure were like angels. My heart was always in Belen."

Nellie graduated from high school in Iowa in 1937 and, as a treat, went to Kansas City to visit an aunt. Her aunt mentioned that Fred Harvey was hiring again. (Nellie's older sister, Olga, had already been hired as a Harvey Girl and was working in Belen.) Nellie decided to apply and was interviewed by Alice Steel. When asked about the interview, Nellie said, "I was scared and Miss Steel knew it. She was so kind!" Nellie was asked if she had experience as a waitress and whether she liked people. "I was truthful about not having waitressing experience, but I lied about my age." Nellie was only seventeen, and the age requirement for a Harvey Girl was eighteen.

Nellie returned home, and according to her daughter, "Mom didn't think a whole lot of it until about three weeks later when she got a crisp white envelope with the Fred Harvey logo embossed on it. Inside the envelope was the offer of a job, a six-month contract and a train pass to Vaughn, New Mexico.

Nellie trained in Vaughn and was then sent to Belen after that Harvey House reopened to serve the troop trains. She also worked at Fray Marcos Harvey Hotel in Williams, Arizona, and was sent to El Tovar in the Grand Canyon and La Fonda in Santa Fe, New Mexico on special assignments. "Our hostess [in Vaughn] was Bertha Jackman, a red head, and she was very strict with us. She always saw that we had a girdle on; not too much makeup; hairnets; and our white skirts, blouses, shoes and stockings were spotless. She even checked our fingernails."

The Harvey staff was expected to be on their best behavior while representing Fred Harvey; however, when not at work, life was relaxed and fun. "Our days were full of fun. We played cards, went on hikes—never got bored." The Harvey employees played croquet on the Harvey House lawn and enjoyed movies at the local movie theater. Nellie remembers that if a Harvey Girl violated a Harvey rule, "the hostesses usually gave them a second chance and Mr. Van, the manager, was quite liberal because he liked to keep the girls that did good work."

Nellie recalls that at the time she became a Harvey Girl, "no blacks, Indians or Mexicans were allowed to work at a Harvey House except in the kitchen, but this changed during the war." Keeping with the customs of the time, black railroad employees and passengers were not allowed to eat in the restaurant. "There was a

Harvey Girls Madge Pinkerton and Wilma Tinker in Belen, New Mexico, 1927. *Courtesy of Belen Harvey House Museum.*

special room for them, but that didn't last too long, and they were soon welcomed in the dining room and lunchroom."

In spite of an offer from Harvey Girls to forfeit their salaries and work only for their room and board and tips, the Belen Harvey House ceased operating in 1939. However, when it reopened during World War II to serve soldiers traveling on troop trains, Nellie, along with other Harvey employees, returned to Belen to serve dozens of trains daily. Later, the building was converted to a Santa Fe Reading Room, and railroad workers most likely boarded in the former Harvey Girl quarters on the second floor.

A familiar Harvey House story: years later, the Belen building was set for demolition. However, in this instance, residents united and created the Harvey House Historic Preservation Project. Citizens signed petitions, wrote letters of support and eventually saved the building. It now houses the Harvey House Museum, and after many years under the intelligent guidance of director Maurine McMillan, it is now part of the City of Belen Public Library system.

Raton

It was a wonderful life. I loved being a Harvey Girl.
—Harvey Girl Opal Hill Sells

Author James P. Bell describes Raton, New Mexico, as the "high and lonesome" sitting on the old "original northern route" of the Santa Fe Railroad through New Mexico. The town may seem remote and lonesome today; however, in its heyday, Raton and nearby Raton Pass (elevation 7,834 feet) were pivotal in the expansion of the railroad. This was the gateway into New Mexico and the West.

Raton Pass was a path over the Sangre de Cristo Mountains for early explorers, trappers and American Indians. It is where one of the first—if not the first—toll roads for covered wagons existed. The Santa Fe Railroad was involved in a controversial brouhaha with another railroad vying for the right to lay tracks at this site. The Santa Fe won, and in 1879, a steam engine burst through the mountains via a manmade tunnel.

The first Harvey House opened in 1882 at a time when Raton was a railroad boomtown. That red two-story wooden structure was replaced in 1903 with

The Santa Fe Depot and Harvey House in Raton, New Mexico. *Courtesy of Michael McMillan.*

an expansive Spanish Mission–style stucco and brick Santa Fe depot and Harvey House with a red tiled roof and a series of trackside arches.

That original Raton Harvey House could be called the birthplace of Harvey Girls. Certainly the *idea* of Harvey Girls began in this tiny New Mexico town. When the Santa Fe railroad came to Raton, a Harvey House was established and an all-male staff served the eating-house patrons, who were mostly miners, cowboys and railroad men. Following an after-hours fight involving the staff, no one was able to work the next morning. When word of the situation reached Fred Harvey, he took the train to Raton to remedy the situation. An enraged Harvey fired everyone and hired a new manager, Tom Gable. Tom proposed replacing the disorderly men with attractive young women, correctly reasoning that the women would be more reliable and cause less trouble. He believed the change in staff would also be well received by train passengers and the community. Harvey agreed. Using popular women's magazines and newspapers, he began advertising for "attractive and intelligent young women eighteen to twenty years of age" to move to the West for employment.

Those first Harvey Girls would not be in Raton for long. Soon after the completion of the new Harvey House and depot, possibly within a year, the restaurant closed. With larger Harvey Houses in Colorado and a little farther down the line in New Mexico, the need for a Harvey restaurant in Raton could not be justified.

Amtrak now uses part of the Raton Harvey House and depot building. Although the distinctive tall spires were removed from the building years ago, the large letters spelling *Raton* still face the tracks, greeting passengers on the Southwest Chief traveling between Chicago and Los Angeles. Several years ago, my daughter and I took Amtrak from Albuquerque to Washington, D.C. It was a memorable trip, but I don't believe we traveled through any scenery more impressive than Raton Pass. Now, because of a decline in freight traffic, BNSF Railway is claiming it cannot maintain the line up to Amtrak's standards, and if this funding deficit isn't resolved, the future of rail transportation through Raton is in jeopardy.

Rincon

It was nice for a young girl to work there because there was no nonsense. They looked after us and took good care of us.
—Harvey Girl Marie Marquez Smiley

This small town along the Rio Grande (near Hatch and north of Las Cruces) had a Harvey House restaurant and a small hotel. The Harvey facilities in Rincon were probably used primarily by railroad employees. Train passengers traveling for business or pleasure were likely to choose a more alluring stop such as El Paso or Albuquerque; however, a hungry passenger of any kind would not pass on the opportunity to enjoy a delicious meal in a Harvey House. Once you entered the plain, two-story wooden structure in Rincon, you were greeted by a horseshoe-shaped counter set with sparkling-clean china and silver. At one end of the counter, next to the large brass cash register, a raised glass case contained cigars, cigarettes and other merchandise usually sold in a Fred Harvey newsstand. Stenciled designs below wide wooden trim, a pressed tin ceiling and framed art on the wall provided visitors with standard Harvey House surroundings.

Rincon plays an important part in my family history, as my grandmother, Gertrude McCormick, was a Harvey Girl in this small Harvey House, and it was there that she met my grandfather. This very personal Harvey Girl story is what set me on the path to pay tribute to the thousands of women who truly civilized the West.

Gertrude Elizabeth McCormick was an orphan who had finished nursing school in Philadelphia and, after working a while, decided

The Santa Fe Depot and two-story Harvey House in Rincon, New Mexico. *Courtesy of Belen Harvey House Museum Photo Archives.*

she wanted to go to Alaska. In early 1912, this would not be an easy accomplishment for a young single woman. Gertrude learned that Fred Harvey was hiring "educated women of good character" to work in his restaurants that stretched from Kansas across the Southwest to California. She recognized an opportunity to work her way toward Alaska, interviewed to be a Harvey Girl and promptly boarded a train to Rincon. I can only imagine the culture shock of leaving a city the size of Philadelphia and landing in this small railroad town in southern New Mexico. However, excitement soon entered Gertrude's life when a tall, dark and very handsome young Frenchman came to town.

At the age of twelve, William Alexander Balmanno left his family on the Island of Mauritius in the Indian Ocean to work on whaling ships. Seventeen years later, he and a friend quit their whaling jobs in Vera Cruz, Mexico, and decided to walk to California. On the way, in Rincon, New Mexico, William took a job with the Santa Fe Railroad to earn money to finish his trip.

The lunch counter in this small Harvey House seated twenty-six, and there was no dining room. Most likely no more than six Harvey Girls worked in Rincon at any one time. The new railroad man who spoke with a heavy French accent must have caused quite a stir. Petite Gertrude caught his attention, and three months later, she and William were married. They spent the rest of their lives in New Mexico, and William worked for the Santa Fe until his retirement.

Manager Claud Sheats went to work for Fred Harvey immediately after World War I was over. "The first pair of long breeches I ever wore, I had on when I went to work for Fred Harvey." Claud painted a humorous picture of life around the remote Rincon Harvey House: "I remember how the burros would come up to the Harvey House to eat when the dinner gong would ring."

Through the years, some stories imply that when New Mexico Harvey Girls caused trouble or couldn't get along with co-workers, they were sent to Rincon as punishment. While I couldn't verify these stories, during my search, I did find several accounts of a Harvey Girl crime spree in 1910 that began in Rincon. Cash and jewelry were taken from a Harvey Girl roommate's trunk, and soon after, an expensive brooch was taken from a Deming Harvey Girl. The thief (and by then ex–Harvey Girl) was caught in Silver City, New Mexico.

The population of Rincon has hovered around two hundred for decades, although just as the expansion of the railroad transportation helped grow the town in the late 1800s, development of a different mode of travel—space travel—may bring new growth to the area. SpaceportAmerica, a site for launching and landing spacecraft, was built just south of Rincon.

The original Harvey House and depot, built in 1883, was destroyed by fire the following year. These buildings were replaced with another wooden depot and two-story Harvey House. The Rincon Harvey House closed in 1933. A one-story structure remains that appears to be part of the 1884 depot.

San Marcial

It was a good experience. I learned you have to give and take in life. If things aren't just exactly like you want, you don't holler too much.
—Harvey Girl Pearl Ramsey

The railroad line stretching from Albuquerque to Deming to El Paso, Texas, included San Marcial and was the Rio Grande Division of the Santa Fe. It was so named because the line followed the river almost the entire route to El Paso. In her book *Horny Toad Man*, author Lenore Dils explains that railroaders preferred to call this line the "Toad" rather than continually refer to the big river that caused them so much grief.

Santa Fe buildings at the division point included a large two-story depot and division office building. Next door, to the south, sat the Harvey House, built in 1883, with seven guest rooms and a lunch counter with seating for twenty-seven.

Harvey House in San Marcial, New Mexico. A vicious flood in 1929 destroyed the Harvey House and the town. *Courtesy of Michael McMillan.*

One Harvey Girl described San Marcial in 1923: "A booming railroad town, a division point on the Santa Fe. San Marcial's Harvey House was two stories high. Right near the station it was. On the first floor was the restaurant. Up above lived the manager and his wife, and about six Harvey Girls."

Throughout its history, San Marcial's location near the Rio Grande proved to be disastrous. Originally established on the east side of the river, a flood destroyed the entire village in 1866, the first of many floods that would plague the community for over sixty years. San Marcial was relocated to the opposite side of the Rio Grande, where the community prospered for a time.

At the beginning of the twentieth century, San Marcial, thirty miles south of Socorro, was the second-largest town in the county and, by 1929, had reached a population of over one thousand. At this time, the town had a bank, a mercantile store, a drugstore, schools, churches and a three-hundred-seat opera house. In the summer of that year, two floods swept through the town in a six-week period. During the second flood, many people took refuge on the second floor of the Harvey House, escaping raging water that washed out fifty-one miles of railroad track and overturned train engines. (Some locals contend that an engine washed downstream and was never found.) No one died from the disaster, but all of San Marcial was destroyed and never rebuilt.

Harvey House entrance in San Marcial, New Mexico. *Courtesy of Luna County Historical Society.*

Twenty-four-year-old Pearl Ramsey was working in a print shop in Wright County, Missouri, in 1923 when a girlfriend told her about the Harvey Girls. "What I did was go up to Springfield, Missouri. When I got there they told me to go up to Kansas City, where a woman interviewed me. She said there was a job for me—in New Mexico! Why, I'd hardly been out of Wright County." Pearl soon boarded a train headed to San Marcial, New Mexico. "San Marcial, you know, was that nice little place flooded out in 1929."

Pearl had never worked in a restaurant, and "some things took getting used to," she explained. "Like, when the men would come in and say 'java.' I honestly didn't know that meant coffee." Pearl remembered only three tables in the dining room. "Mostly I worked at the big lunch counter. At first I was on a split shift—2:00 p.m. to 10:00 p.m. Then, when the head waitress, Margaret Sampson was her name, got married, I moved up to Margaret's job and worked days." Pearl, who earned one dollar per day in the Missouri print shop, was thrilled with the sixty dollars per month plus room and board and laundry she was promised as a Harvey Girl. "Actually, I got about ninety dollars a month with tips." The pay was better, but life as a Harvey Girl had restrictions. "You had to be in by 10:00 p.m., and no late dates. We had to clean the drinking glasses, and they had to sparkle. And of course, the customer was always right." Pearl blames later trouble with her feet on her Harvey Girl days. "The only time you sat down was to fold napkins or polish silverware. You worked real hard. They held a train until everybody got through eating."

Pearl married a Santa Fe telegraph operator, William Ramsey, and soon after, he was transferred to nearby Rincon, New Mexico. "They had a Harvey House in Rincon, but my husband didn't want me to work anymore, so I didn't. So I really was a Harvey Girl for only about a year. But it was a good experience. I learned you have to give and take in life. If things aren't just exactly like you want, you don't holler too much."

"So many girls, like I was, couldn't afford to travel and see the world," Pearl said. "We didn't see the world, but we saw the West and parts of the country we would not have seen."

Five years after Pearl and her husband left San Marcial, the floods came. Harvey Girl Judy Serna, a San Marcial native, was working at the small but efficient Harvey House during the floods of 1929. The first reaction when the second, more severe flood hit was to escape by train, but the bridge was washed out, and trains weren't going anywhere. Judy remembered that the calm manner with which the Harvey House manager, Mr. Coverdale, reacted to the situation helped keep the Harvey House employees calm. The group waited out the storm on the second floor, where they drank free Cokes and ate food hastily brought up from the kitchen during their escape from the rising waters. High-water marks can be seen in photos of the depot and Harvey House taken after the flood, showing four to five feet of water throughout the town and leaving at least a foot of mud behind. In some areas, houses were buried to the roofline in silt.

There are two versions of the rescue the following morning, one involving a large motorboat from Elephant Butte, a nearby lake. Another described a local cowboy riding his horse through the deep water, making many trips to carry those stranded in the Harvey House to safety. Personally, I like the second version. It would make a better movie.

Following the flood of 1929, the Santa Fe abolished the division point and abandoned the roundhouse. The Harvey House was closed and the building demolished; most employees were reassigned to nearby Harvey Houses. In 1936, the Santa Fe depot was moved to Hatch, New Mexico.

Chapter 5

NEWS AND SMOKES

Harvey Newsstand

Las Cruces

Las Cruces is the second-largest city in New Mexico (Albuquerque is the largest); however, it was not a major railroad crossroads, and the only Fred Harvey business there was a newsstand. Typically a newsstand would offer items such as tobacco products and candy as well as newspapers from major U.S. cities and the much-desired Fred Harvey picture postcards. In larger railroad centers, there might be a newsstand inside the restaurant, depot or in the Harvey hotel lobby as well as a portable newsstand that was rolled out closer to the tracks. The Las Cruces newsstand opened in 1910 inside the depot facing the tracks. The colorful display of goods was designed to attract passengers off the train.

Customer service in a Harvey newsstand was treated as seriously as in restaurants and hotels. Although local young men might be hired to handle operations during less busy times, each newsstand was assigned a Harvey-trained manager who made sure operations were up to the Harvey standard.

The postcard business flourished after 1904, when Ford Harvey began working with the Detroit Publishing Company, which had developed a process for colorizing black-and-white photos. A good number of the postcards from the early Harvey days have survived and are often offered online. Many of the images in this book were digitized from original Harvey postcards from the private collection of Michael McMillan.

A Fred Harvey newsstand inside the Santa Fe Depot in Las Cruces, New Mexico, sold tobacco products, newspapers and sundries to train passengers. *Courtesy of Michael McMillan.*

The Las Cruces Santa Fe depot closed in 1966. I was unable to find the year when the Harvey newsstand closed; however, throughout the Harvey system, many of these thriving kiosks survived long after lunchrooms and dining rooms had closed. The Las Cruces Railroad Museum is now housed in the Mission Revival–style Santa Fe depot.

Chapter 6

LONG AGO

Early Harvey Houses

Coolidge

There was only a lunchroom at the Harvey House in Coolidge, a small town site twenty miles east of Gallup, that opened in 1885. In the 1880s, when a main railroad line was built through the town, the name was changed from Crane in honor of Thomas Jefferson Coolidge, a director of the Atlantic and Pacific Railroad.

I found very little information on this New Mexico Harvey House except a reference indicating the surroundings and food service did not meet Harvey standards. After a visit, Fred Harvey noted that the pastry was poor, the coffee was poor and the house was generally poor.

Herman Schweizer, a young German immigrant who had earned a good reputation within the Harvey company, was dispatched to solve the problem. Herman was only sixteen, but he successfully improved the quality of food and service. However, as railroad activity declined in the small town, the need for an eating house also diminished and the Harvey House closed in 1889. In his free time at Coolidge, the young man rode horseback through the nearby Navajo and Hopi reservations. Herman developed relationships with the native artisans and purchased jewelry, blankets and other handcrafted items that he in turn sold to customers at the Harvey House. This experience would be the foundation for the very successful Harvey Indian Department.

Near Fort Wingate, Coolidge was once a busy trade center with a livery stable, two general stores and several saloons. Soon after the railroad division point was moved to Gallup at the end of the nineteenth century, a fire destroyed most of the buildings in Coolidge and the town never recovered.

Wallace

One of the early New Mexico Harvey Houses, the Wallace Harvey House was on Santo Domino Pueblo land approximately one hundred miles west of Las Vegas, New Mexico. The two-story wooden building opened in 1883 with lodging facilities and a laundry and closed a decade later. Wallace was the nearest Harvey House to Albuquerque, and as that city's railroad facilities grew, Wallace declined. Within ten years, the buildings were abandoned and the Harvey House closed.

Chapter 7

FRED'S FRIENDS

Keeping the History Alive

The influence of Fred Harvey continues almost 140 years after his handshake with the head of the Santa Fe Railroad. While working on this book, I have become acquainted with a diverse group of folks who continue to preserve and share the history of Fred Harvey, Harvey Houses and the company's extensive reach.

It is surprising where this Fred Harvey influence surfaces. I recently read a printed piece about singer Pharrell Williams. Williams, who is best known for his "happy" music and oversized Smokey the Bear hat, has designed a line of leather, locomotive-themed handbags for the exclusive French label Maynot. In the interview, he was asked where he got the idea for the handbags, and Williams explained, "For about seven or eight years I had wanted to make these bags after seeing *The Harvey Girls* with Judy Garland." Beyonce owns one of the train-shaped bags, and you can too! Just might need to save your pennies, because these Fred Harvey–inspired bags range in price from $4,000 to $10,000.

About midway through my research for this book, I discovered Danyelle Gentry Petersen. That discovery led me to her father, Skip Gentry, who is clearly a frontrunner for having the largest collection of Fred Harvey memorabilia ever. Telephone conversations with Danyelle (usually while she was driving in the California sun) always left me smiling. When I met her and her brother Beau Gentry in person, I was impressed by their sincerity and obvious appreciation for something so dear to their father: all things Fred Harvey.

Skip Gentry with a few pieces from his extensive collection of Fred Harvey memorabilia. Items from the collection are part of a Fred Harvey exhibit at New Mexico History Museum in Santa Fe. *Courtesy of Skip Gentry's Fred Harvey Memorabilia Collection.*

Unfortunately, Skip Gentry passed away in 2010. However, through the efforts of his two children, Skip's enthusiasm and energy lives on through his collection. Skip was a lifelong resident of California's San Fernando Valley and worked in the motion picture industry as a driver for forty years. For years, the collector was the go-to guy for Fred Harvey questions, and his eye for authentic collectible items was well known.

We can assume Skip's interest in collecting was influenced by his mother, who owned the first antique store in Van Nuys, California. When asked what started her father on this lifelong pursuit of Harvey memorabilia, Danyelle explained, "He started collecting Indian items when he was about seven years old. So that was a long career of collecting and learning for sixty years. It was also because of his love of all Indian cultures and the beauty of the Southwest."

Skip was described by his peers as "a legendary collector of antiques, Native American Indian Art, Fred Harvey memorabilia and friends." He had an old, rubber shower curtain from a Fred Harvey hotel in his bathroom and used replica Harvey House china because his ten-piece collection "of the real thing" was too precious. In a 1993 interview for a local newspaper, Skip admitted he once dated two modern-day Harvey Girls and counted several more as good friends. He described his collection as "a link to a simpler time, a better time, a romantic time."

Pieces from Skip's collection have been featured in museums in the Southwest. Many items from his five-thousand-plus piece Fred Harvey collection are part of "Setting the Standard: The Fred Harvey Company and Its Legacy," an exhibit that opened in 2014 at the New Mexico History Museum in Santa Fe, New Mexico.

Everet Apodaca grew up in Las Vegas, New Mexico, and first became intrigued with the Fred Harvey legacy when he was in junior high school. The Montezuma Harvey hotel was vacant, with broken windows and unlocked doors. Everet and his friends would go to the hot springs near the Montezuma and then venture into the old building. "We were just kids exploring, but I was fascinated by the grandeur of that structure." He began to read about the Santa Fe Railroad and Harvey Houses and later began collecting related items. "At the time I learned we had another Harvey House in Las Vegas [the Castaneda] no one went to Railroad Avenue where it was located. Everything was boarded up. I couldn't understand how these grand hotels had been part of my hometown." Through the years, "many things came my way, and my collection grew so large, eventually I had to sell some pieces." With the renewed interest in Fred Harvey due to the renovation of the Castaneda, Everet is rediscovering his collection and its ties to his hometown. He recently re-created Harvey Girl uniforms for the Las Vegas Harvey Girls to wear for special events and to conduct tours of the Castaneda and Montezuma. Everet is a dealer at Rough Rider Antiques, just a few blocks from the Castaneda, where he offers Santa Fe Railroad– and Fred Harvey–related items for sale. "I buy, sell and trade to buy the next piece."

Fred's friends are not just collectors of Harvey memorabilia; many are also dedicated to preserving and sharing Fred Harvey history. Kathy Hendrickson and her husband, Bill, chose Las Vegas, New Mexico, as a place to retire a few years ago. (They moved from Kuwait and restored a wonderful Victorian home. Theirs is an interesting story but too long to share here. Ask me about it the next time we talk.)

"I love history and historical buildings," Kathy explained. "That interest is one thing that drew us to Las Vegas." (Over nine hundred buildings in Las Vegas are on the National Register of Historic Places.) Kathy enjoyed

Blue Chain Fred Harvey china and a silver pitcher that were used at the Castaneda in Las Vegas, New Mexico. *Courtesy of Everet Apodaca.*

walking in her new hometown, especially on Railroad Avenue, where she discovered the Castaneda. "I took a lot of photos. The Castaneda is such an interesting and lovely building," she said. "I researched the hotel while also researching the house we bought. That's when I learned the Castaneda had been a Harvey House." Kathy hadn't heard of Fred Harvey, and with her increased knowledge of his legacy, she became more intrigued. "One day, Bill and I went to the depot here in Las Vegas and took the train to Winslow, Arizona, to visit La Posada." A sister hotel to the Castaneda and other Harvey luxury hotels, La Posada was purchased by Allan Affeldt almost twenty years ago and has been completely restored.

Through her research efforts, Kathy became involved with the Las Vegas Citizens Committee for Historic Preservation and historic home tours sponsored by the group. Her desire to share the Fred Harvey history led to a discussion with Allan Affeldt, the new owner of the Castaneda. At his suggestion, Kathy organized the Las Vegas Harvey Girls: Pam Beuthe, Dee Clark, Martha Johnsen, Becky Johnson and Virginia West. This group of women, dressed in traditional Harvey Girl black-and-white uniforms and led by Hendrickson, who wears the attire of an Indian Detour Courier, conduct tours of the Castaneda and the Montezuma and assist with events promoting the heritage of Las Vegas.

The Las Vegas Harvey Girls, led by Detour Courier Kathy Hendrickson (center), take an active role in preserving and sharing Fred Harvey history in Las Vegas, New Mexico. *Author's collection.*

Kathy and Jim Weir are shown relaxing on a stairway in La Fonda in Santa Fe, New Mexico. The couple, who lives in Arizona, are avid Fred Harvey and Mary Colter fans. *Author's collection.*

Former Harvey Girls Bernette Jarvis and Beverly Ireland are pictured with a poster promoting a Fred Harvey exhibit at the New Mexico History Museum. The poster features the twins when they worked at La Fonda in Santa Fe in 1955. *Courtesy of Kathy Weir.*

It has been surprising to me how much the research and writing about Harvey Girls has enriched my life beyond the finished product—published books. One example is the warm friendship I now enjoy with Jim and Kathy Weir. The couple enjoys traveling, so it makes perfect sense that while on a trip to the last Harvey House built—La Posada in Winslow, Arizona—they discovered the story of Fred Harvey. In the gift shop at La Posada, Kathy bought books about Mary Colter, the architect who completed twenty-one projects for the Fred Harvey company. After realizing the strong connection between Colter and Fred Harvey, it was a natural progression to collect books about Fred Harvey. As Jim and Kathy explored Harvey House locations, their interest in the subject grew, leading Kathy to create a Fred Harvey/Mary Colter Fan Club Facebook page. The page is now a smart intersection of interesting Harvey facts and the sharing of current events pertaining to Harvey and Colter. The Weirs hosted a breakfast in La Plazuela dining room at La Fonda for members of the fan club who were in Santa Fe for the opening of the new exhibit "Setting the Standard: The Fred Harvey Company and Its Legacy" at the New Mexico History Museum.

Chapter 8

HARVEY HOUSE KITCHENS

Original Recipes

Quality customer service by Harvey Girls in Fred Harvey restaurants was a major factor in the success of America's first fast-food business, but that was only half of the story. The restaurants also prospered because of the quality and variety of freshly prepared food that was consistent all along the Santa Fe line.

Following are a few personal recipes used by John Frenden, who was the chef at the Alvarado in Albuquerque and La Fonda in Santa Fe. They are presented here as he wrote them. Note that Chef Frenden's recipes only include ingredients. Experience told him everything else he needed to know. The collection of original, handwritten recipes is held at the Belen Harvey House Museum in Belen, New Mexico.

APPLE CAKE

2 cups flour

1¾ cup sugar

1 oil

3 eggs

1 teaspoon soda

¼ salt

½ cinnamon

4—6 apples, peeled

SAUERKRAUT CAKE.

½ cp BUTTER

1½ " SUGAR

2 " FLOUR

½ " COCO POWDER

3 - EGGS

1. TSP. B. P.

1 T " B. SODA

1 Cp WATER

VANILLA - ¼ T. SALT

Icing

1 ⅓ cp SAUERKRAUT - RINSED + CUT

6 OZ CHOC. CHIPS - MELTED

4 TSP. BUTTER

VANILLA - SALT

½ cp. SOUR CREAM

Harvey House chef John Frenden's handwritten Sauerkraut Cake recipe. *Courtesy of Belen Harvey House Museum.*

Harvey House Kitchens

Cornbread [for a crowd]

24 pounds flour
12 pounds cornmeal
6 gallons milk
24 ounces B.P. [baking powder]
36 eggs
4 pounds shortening

Bread (1 loaf)

3 ounces yeast
3 pounds flour
1 quart milk
6 ounces lard melted
6 ounces sugar
1 ounces salt

Donuts

1 pound flour
¼ pound sugar
2 ounces butter or pinch salt
Tablespoon lemon extract
¾ ounces B.P. [baking powder]
2 eggs
½ pint milk

Yorkshire Pudding

10 eggs
5 cups milk
5 tablespoons salt
5 cups flour
2½ cups beef dripping

Here are recipes included in a booklet distributed to Santa Fe Railroad passengers as a marketing piece emphasizing the dedication of the Santa Fe and the Fred Harvey system, which "worked together to provide good food to all who come our way."

For this "side trip adventure in cooking," recipes were presented in cooking terms familiar to the non-professional chef and in quantities most useful for home consumption.

HUEVOS RANCHEROS
Chef Konrad Allgaier
La Fonda, Santa Fe, New Mexico

1 cup pinto beans
1 tablespoon red chili powder
4 tablespoons minced onion
½ to 1 teaspoon finely minced green chili pepper
¼ cup water
2 tablespoons butter
2 eggs
1 teaspoon butter

Wash beans, cover with cold water and let soak overnight. In the morning, heat to boiling, reduce heat and let simmer, covered, until beans are tender 3 or 4 hours. Cool. Add red chili powder, which may be obtained from Mexican grocery store, to the cold water and let soak one hour. Sauté onion and very finely minced green chili pepper in butter very slowly until tender but not browned. Add beans that have been broken up coarsely with a fork and heat through. Add ¼ to ½ cup hot water if beans are too dry. Transfer heated beans to a well-buttered shirred egg dish or individual casserole. Make two depressions in top of beans using back of tablespoon, and drop an egg in each depression. Pour 2 tablespoons soaked red chili powder over the top and dot top of eggs with butter. Bake in a moderate oven (350 degrees), 20 to 25 minutes or until eggs are set sufficiently. Yield: 1 serving.

LA FONDA PUDDING

Chef Konrad Allgaier
La Fonda, Santa Fe, New Mexico

3 egg yolks
1 cup sugar
1 cup finely crushed graham crackers (12)
½ cup chopped walnuts
1 teaspoon baking powder
⅛ teaspoon salt
½ teaspoon vanilla
3 egg whites, stiffly beaten
heavy cream

Beat egg yolks until thick and lemon-colored; gradually add sugar, beating constantly. Fold in graham crackers, chopped nuts, baking powder, salt and vanilla. Fold in beaten egg whites. Bake in a buttered 8- by 8- by 2-inch pan in moderate oven (350 degrees) for 45 minutes. Cool in pan for 10 minutes. Remove from pan. Cut in squares and serve topped with whipped cream and extra chopped walnuts if desired.

PORK CHOPS BAVARIAN

Chef John Frenden
Alvarado Hotel, Albuquerque, New Mexico

6 thick pork chops
1½ pounds raw sauerkraut
1 medium-sized onion, diced
1 clove garlic
salt and pepper to taste
1 teaspoon sugar
1 whole bay leaf
1 pound canned tomatoes
6 raw potatoes, thickly sliced

Brown pork chops in skillet, remove and put sauerkraut, onion, clove of garlic, salt, pepper, sugar and bay leaf in pan; pour tomatoes over this. Arrange thick slices of raw potatoes around skillet. Lay pork chops on top and cover with lid. Simmer for 1 hour.

BIBLIOGRAPHY

Bell, James B. *Ghost Trains: Images from America's Railroad Heritage*. New York: Chartwell Books, 2014.

Dugan, Brenna Stewart. "Girls Wanted: For Service at the Fred Harvey Houses." Graduate thesis, Texas Tech University, December 2008.

Foster, George H., and Peter C. Weiglin. *The Harvey House Cookbook*. Atlanta, GA: Longstreet Press, 1992.

Fried, Stephen. *Appetite for America: Fred Harvey and the Business of Civilizing the Wild West—One Meal at a Time*. New York: Random House, Inc., 2010.

Grattan, Virginia L. *Mary Colter: Builder Upon the Red Earth*. Flagstaff, AZ: Northland Press, 1980.

Henderson, James D. *Meals by Fred Harvey: A Phenomenon of the American West*. Fort Worth: Texas Christian University Press, 1969.

Howard, Kathleen L., and Diana F. Pardue. *Inventing the Southwest: The Fred Harvey Company and Native American Art*. Flagstaff, AZ: Northland Publishing, 1998.

Latimer, Rosa Walston. *Harvey Houses of Texas: Historic Hospitality from the Gulf Coast to the Panhandle*. Charleston, SC: The History Press, 2014.

Marshall, James. *Santa Fe: The Railroad that Built an Empire*. New York: Random House, 1945.

Melzer, Richard. *Fred Harvey Houses of the Southwest*. Charleston, SC: Arcadia Publishing, 2008.

Poling-Kempes, Lesley. *The Harvey Girls: Women Who Opened the West*. New York: Paragon House, 1989.

Riskin, Marci L. *The Train Stops Here: New Mexico's Railway Legacy*. Albuquerque: University of New Mexico Press, 2005.

Slaney, Deborah C. *Jewel of the Railroad Era: Albuquerque's Alvarado Hotel*. Albuquerque, NM: Albuquerque Museum, 2009.

Thomas, Diane. *The Southwestern Indian Detours*. Phoenix, AZ: Hunter Publishing, 2002.

INDEX

INDEX

V

Valdes, John 9
Vaughn, New Mexico 20, 55, 101, 110
Veley, Nellie Berg 45, 110

W

Wallace, New Mexico 124
Warren, Aslaug Helene Schau 41
Weir, Jim and Kathy 10, 130
Williams, Pharrell 125
Willis, Ethel Irby 54
Wimmer, Steve 83
Wister, Owen 67, 69

Z

Zinn, Frank 85
Zuellig, Charlie 32

ABOUT THE AUTHOR

Rosa Walston Latimer owns an independent bookstore and is a playwright and an award-winning photographer. She has written for national and regional magazines and newspapers and was news editor of a print and an online newspaper and supervising director of a nationally syndicated television program.

The story of her Harvey Girl grandmother sparked her interest in preserving women's history. After being told by a museum curator in another state that there were no Harvey Houses in Texas, she was determined to preserve this important part of the state's railroad history and inspired to write her first book, *Harvey Houses of Texas: Historic Hospitality from the Gulf Coast to the Panhandle*. This book was nominated for the 2016 TCU Texas Book Award. Now Latimer has chronicled her grandmother's story as well as the story of many other New Mexico Harvey Girls in her second book, *Harvey Houses of New Mexico: Historic Hospitality from Raton to Deming*. While working on these books, she realized the Kansas Harvey story should be told—after all, Kansas is where the Harvey House story began. Latimer's third book in the

Harvey House series, *Harvey Houses of Kansas: Historic Hospitality from Topeka to Syracuse* was chosen by the Kansas State Librarian for a 2016 Notable Kansas Book Award.

The author lives above her bookstore in a two-story, historic building. She shares the upstairs space with her three rescue dogs: Muffin, Penny and Ally. Downstairs, the bookstore cat, Ruby, happily greets customers and watches the traffic on Main Street. Rosa is actively involved in the arts and historical preservation of her community, and gallery space in her bookstore features regional artists. She is currently working on a book about three significant historic hotels in Las Vegas, New Mexico, and has begun research for a fourth book in the Harvey House series.